I REBUKE THEE

CONFRONTING THE DEVIL YOU KNOW

VINCENT WOODS

SECUREITZ

I Rebuke Thee

This title is also available as an e-book. Visit www.amazon.com/e-book.

This title is also available at www.irebukethee.com.

Requests for information should be addressed to: www.secureitz.com.

Requests can also be made at www.irebukethee@gmail.com.

All Scripture quotations are taken from The Holy Bible, King James' translation (Public Domain). Any internet addresses (websites, etc.) and telephone numbers in this book are offered as a resource. They are not intended in any way to be or imply an endorsement by said resources.

Cover design: Art Infinity

Printed in the United States of America

ISBN: 979-8-8684640-7-2

The hand of the Lord was upon me,
and carried me out in the spirit of
the Lord, and set me down in the midst
of the valley which was full of bones,
And caused me to pass by them
round about: and, behold, there were
very many in the open valley; and,
lo, they were very dry. And he said unto me,
Son of man, can these bones live? And I
answered, O Lord God, thou knowest.
Again he said unto me, Prophesy upon
these bones, and say unto them, O ye
dry bones, hear the word of the Lord.
Thus saith the Lord God unto these bones;
Behold, I will cause breath to enter into
you, and ye shall live:
(Ezekiel 37:1-5)

What can a Son say to a loving Mother that has not been said? How about this? Mom thank you for introducing me to Jesus. He is everything you said he would be and much more.

From the Author

I have developed a two-prong approach for distributing my book. I fully understand that there are cost factors to consider, so I am selling my book at a reasonable price. However, I am well aware that there are many who need to read the book but rarely purchase a book. With this in mind, I plan to give the book away free to community centers, nursing homes, and shelters. If you would like to help me spread the Gospel and donate my book to those in need, please visit the book's website and choose the gift button. This will buy a book for the less fortunate in our community. Your donation is tax deductible. Thank you. Rev. Vincent Woods.

Also, I would love to hear your thoughts on the book. Good, bad, or indifferent.

And if you have any ideas about my next book. I would love to hear from you. I am leaning toward (I Rebuke Thee Confronting the Lack of Faith)

Contact me at www.irebukethee@gmail.com or www.irebukethee.com

TABLE OF CONTENTS

I REBUKE THEE

PREFACE

"And it shall come to pass in the last days, saith God, I will pour out of my Spirit upon all flesh: and your sons and your daughters shall prophesy, and your young men shall see visions, and your old men shall dream dreams:" (Acts 2:17).

If you are reading this book, it means the experience I had in the early morning hours of March 18th was a message from the Lord. If not, it was just the disturbance of sleep and a partial dream sequence caused by a late-night sandwich made with questionable Mayonnaise. If it is the latter, this book has joined the two others; I never quite got around to finishing. And if that is the case, I have truly learned the meaning of "hold the mayo." So, hopefully, you are now reading this my first book. If you are, I suggest you do as the Apostle Paul instructed the Church in Ephesus and Suit Up. "Put on the whole armour of God, that ye may be able to stand against the wiles of the devil. 12 For we wrestle not against flesh and blood, but against principalities, against powers, against the rulers of the darkness of this world, against spiritual wickedness in high places." (Ephesians 6:11-12).

Many people will regard my opening statement as questionable, sinner and saint alike. After all, who in their right mind talks with or receives a message from God? Well, I stand guilty as charged. And, if I am being candid, I talk to God all the time. If you want to know why and how? It is called Prayer. Most of us were naively taught that praying is something you do on Sunday at Church. Or at least what you do at the end of the day, in the privacy of your own home, kneeling beside your bed. All of this is true, but prayer does not have to be restricted to just those places. Prayer can be done anywhere, at any time, and any place. Prayer is simply sincere communication with God. While driving to work or sitting in a classroom at school, you can pray. Maybe you are taking a leisurely walk through your neighborhood and decide to say hi to God. Let me be the first to say that you, my friend, have just prayed. Prayer is a spiritual form of communication, and we all know communication is a two-way street. This means not only does God hear you, he may very well answer you and say "hi" back. "Also I heard the voice of the Lord, saying, Whom shall I send, and who will go for us? Then said I, Here am I; send me." (Isaiah 6:8).

God talks to us all. Unfortunately, most cannot distinguish between His voice and all of the other voices and distractions that are present. "And he said, Go forth, and stand upon the mount before the Lord. And, behold, the Lord passed by, and a great and strong wind rent the mountains, and brake in pieces the rocks before the Lord; but the Lord was not in the wind: and after the wind an earthquake; but the Lord was not in the earthquake: 12 And after the earthquake a fire; but the Lord was not in the fire: and after the fire a still small voice. 13 And it was so, when Elijah heard it, that he wrapped his face in his mantle, and went out, and stood in the entering in of the cave. And, behold, there came a voice unto him, and said, What doest thou here, Elijah?" (1 Kings 19:11-13). We have all seen movies where the hero hears from God in a booming voice that shakes the Earth. In reality, God's voice is usually much more-subtle. It is the voice you hear in your subconscious. The small voice that tells you not to do something you know is wrong. Or it is the voice that tells you to do something good for someone just because. People have often misidentified the still, small voice of God. They use terms such as. "My second mind told me." or "My first thought was." and, "I should have listened to the little voice in my head.". Often, this is God talking.

And I am bringing you good tidings of great joy because God is and will speak to you. If you are willing to hear and listen. "My son, if thou wilt receive my words, and hide my commandments with thee; 2 So that thou incline thine ear unto wisdom, and apply thine heart to understanding; 5 Then shalt thou understand the fear of the Lord, and find the knowledge of God." (Proverbs 2:1-2,5).

As you may have now discovered, this book is not about Christian Prosperity. I cannot show you how to pray your way into financial well-being in seven easy steps. I don't think God would have awakened me for that; an email would have sufficed. If you are seeking Spiritual advice on how to be blessed with a Mansion in Beverly Hills, this is not the book, and I am not your guy. However, if you seek to hear Servant, well done when you reach the end of this Earthly Journey. And you want to move into a house not built by man's hands. I can most definitely help you achieve those goals. I must admit I have doubts about the success of this book. I wonder if it will be well received. The reason being this book is going to shine the Light of God on some dark areas within the Faith. We are going to take a long critical look at Christians and Christianity. And, unfortunately, it is not a pretty picture. One thing this book is not. It is not your typical Christian literature that has pacified the Faith in recent years. What this book will do, starting with chapter one - **How Did We Get Here,** and chapter two - **The Fight Begins**, is help you understand where we are as a Faith and where we need to be in these tumultuous times. Chapter three - **Collateral Damage** will expose the harm that can be done to you, or others, because of someone else's actions. Chapter four - **The Devil You Know,** will help you identify your adversary, the Devil, even if that Devil is you. Chapter five - **The Devil in Disguise,** will teach you how to identify

Satan and his Minions. As well as identify the tactics, he uses against the Children of God. Chapter six - **The Spirit of The Matter,** will show and help you get true Spiritual understanding. Chapter seven - **The Power of The Tongue,** will teach Believers what to say and what not to say. Chapter eight - **Jesus Or Adam Not Both,** will show Believers we cannot serve two Masters. Chapter nine - **The Kingdom of Heaven** will teach you how to gain entrance into the right Kingdom. The final chapter - **The End Is Near,** will help you prepare for what's to come.

This book will reveal the tools and resources our Father God has given His Children. Holy instruments that are now made available to Christians which will allow us to defeat our enemy, Satan. If necessary, this book will show you how to take corrective actions against any behavior not befitting a Child of God. I truly believe God called me to write this book so it can serve as another weapon within the Christian Arsenal. A new weapon that will help followers of Christ Jesus emerge victorious in this fight we call life. We, as Believers are entering into the final battles of a War that started in the Garden of Eden. God needs Soldiers that will be steadfast and irremovable for such a time as this. "For if thou altogether holdest thy peace at this time, then shall there enlargement and deliverance arise to the Jews from another place; but thou and thy father's house shall be destroyed: and who knoweth whether thou art come to the kingdom for such a time as this?" (Esther 4:14).

We will start with a detailed look at an Individual and Subject Matter that has not been examined to the degree of importance it surely deserves. We will discuss a character that is so Enigmatic that there is little reference to him in today's Society. I will also point out how this Individual is slowly becoming a footnote in the annals of the Church. This troubles me to my core. It was my fear of this Individual that drove me to Jesus. The love I now have for Christ came sometime later in life. This person is not the subject of any scandalous tweets. He has never gone viral, nor has he ever trended. Yet, he is the single source of all of humanity's afflictions. Every betrayal, every account of violence, every murder, every lie, every war. In our world, any form of evil throughout history can be traced back to this Individual. Who, pray tell could this be? Is it Adolf Hitler? Could it be Jezebel? Or how about Alexander the Great? The answer is yes; he was the driving force behind each of those and many more bad individuals. However, neither of them is our Super Villain. He's something much more Malevolent. He is evil Incarnate. The Individual I am speaking of is the Devil, Satan himself, and all the Hellfire he has to offer. There you have it. I have said his name out loud, with all seriousness and conviction. Now that I have said the name of Satan and put it in print. I can hear the snide remarks made by people who are too intelligent to believe in such Fairy Tales. The looks of utter contempt, along with a hefty reply of - "are you kidding me?". Yes, I know it is hard to believe, but I want to have an intellectual conversation about the Devil. And hopefully try to determine how did we get here as a people?

The Bible is the most printed and read book in all of history. Billions of people believe in God, and billions more have died believing they will spend Eternity in His presence. My parents and grandparents are counted in that number. They are currently enjoying Heaven's many splendors and glory. "After this I beheld, and, lo, a great multitude, which no man could number, of all nations, and kindreds, and people, and tongues, stood before the throne, and before the Lamb, clothed with white robes, and palms in their hands;" (Revelation 7:9). I too believe that one day, I will be reunited with my family gathered around the Throne of the Almighty.

Christians all understand that the Bible is God's absolute undeniable Holy Word. With this understanding, how is it possible that the main Antagonist in the Bible has managed to remove himself from the Human Collective? The name Satan appears forty-nine times in the King James Bible. His less formal name, the Devil, comes in at a whopping forty-five times. Along with a host of other aliases. Yet, he has skirted any real implications regarding human affairs. The demon who ruined Paradise. The one being who threatened Creation itself. Satan is responsible for the divide between humanity and God. A divide that still exists to this very day. Please give this some thought. In the Synoptic Gospels of Matthew, Mark, and Luke. There are scriptures that describe how Satan tried to tempt our Lord and Savior. Satan had the unmitigated gall to demand Jesus yield to his evil authority. "And saith unto him, If thou be the Son of God, cast thyself down: for it is written, He shall give his angels charge concerning thee: and in their hands they shall bear thee up, lest at any time thou dash thy foot against a stone." (Matthew 4:6). "And he was there in the wilderness forty days, tempted of Satan; and was with the wild beasts; and the angels ministered unto him." (Mark 1:13). "If thou therefore wilt worship me, all shall be thine." (Luke 4:7). With all this Holy evidence, how has Satan clouded Humanities Mind? So much so that the very mentioning of his name makes the speaker of said name an utter laughingstock. The subject of ridicule and scorn. What Firm handles the Devil's PR? In the early days of Christianity, “the Devil made me do it” was a plausible defense. Howbeit, you were still burned at the stake or hanged, but people believed you. As your untimely demise indicated. Fast forward to modern times, and you will find no one ever says the Devil made me do it. Although now more so than ever, it is quite evident that he did. The phrase has joined the ranks of other non-plausible statements that Mankind has long since abandoned.

(e.g., The Butler did it. It's not what it looks like. The dog ate my homework.).

There you have it. The who, what, and why of a restless night spent with God. It is my sincere belief. Through the inspired pages of this Book, the Holy Spirit will provide the necessary knowledge and wisdom needed for such an evil time as this. "But the Comforter, which is the Holy Ghost, whom the Father will send in my name, he shall teach you all things, and bring all things to your remembrance, whatsoever I have said unto you." (John 14:26).

Good morning readers; it is confirmed you will enjoy this book. It turns out it was not the mayo. It is 5 a.m. on the morning of June 1st, and the Spirit of God woke me at 3 a.m., and boy, our Father had a lot to say. Several chapters are already written, and there are many more forthcoming. I repeat, it was not the mayo. Although that Memorial-day potato salad was made with mayo, I'm sure that's just a coincidence. Anyway, I am going back to bed because I need to buy a thumb drive to back up my laptop later today.

Also, a couple of housekeeping issues. All scripture quotes for my book will come from the King James Bible. It has served me quite well for many years. The King James Bible has proven to be a reliable reference source for the accurate translation of the Original Text. I am also aware the King James Bible can be difficult to read and navigate because it is written in an antiquated language. You will notice some words are spelled differently, or the meaning has changed. But rest assured, through the impartation of the Holy Spirit. I will interpret God's compelling Word in plain, easily understood terminology. "For the Holy Ghost shall teach you in the same hour what ye ought to say." (Luke 12:12).

My methodology will consist of me making a point and then verifying that point with a Scripture. Here's an example. Because of technological advancements, many Believers worship at home and choose not to attend in person Church Service. Although it is convenient, they miss the significant benefits of true worship with other Believers in the House of God. "And let us consider one another to provoke unto love and to good works: 25 Not forsaking the assembling of ourselves together, as the manner of some is; but exhorting one another: and so much the more, as ye see the day approaching." (Hebrews 10:24-25).

As you have read, I strongly believe in prayer, and I know from personal experience any time you take on the Devil - he fights dirty. So, I am asking you to please pray a hedge of protection around me and my family as I continue to travel the path God has laid before me. Just in case you are wondering, how can I ask for prayer from people who have not yet read the book? It is not a blunder, although it does seem that I am putting the cart before the proverbial horse. Trust me; it will make sense later.

"Confess your faults one to another, and pray one for another, that ye may be healed. The effectual fervent prayer of a righteous man availeth much." (James 5:16).

INTRODUCTION

"Be sober, be vigilant; because your adversary the devil, as a roaring lion, walketh about, seeking whom he may devour:" (1 Peter 5:8).

Welcome back; by now you should have noticed my Writing Style is somewhat lighthearted. I purposely chose this style because it is very close to my personality. Also, I have discovered that after twenty years of preaching and teaching, people are more attentive and engaged in my Sermons or Bible Studies if they can laugh or smile once in a while. However, this does not lessen the seriousness of the subject matter. All Christians can attest that Satan is not to be taken lightly. The Bible tells us that he is here for one purpose and one purpose only. "The thief cometh not, but for to steal, and to kill, and to destroy:" (John 10:10a). In short, he wants to make our lives and afterlives a living Hell. The second part of that verse is stated. "I am come that they might have life, and that they might have it more abundantly." (John 10:10b). As you can easily see, based on this scripture. The only way mankind can avoid certain destruction is through our Lord and Savior, Jesus Christ.

Hear me and hear me well; as stated by the previous scripture, this is a matter of Life and Death. My fellow Believers, this is for all the Marbles. The Devil is real, and he commands demons to do his bidding. Those very demons are indwelled within many people and individuals you may have contact with daily. Please understand a demon's main purpose is to destroy its Host. And anyone else it interacts with that is not covered by the Blood of Jesus. Have you noticed that minor altercations or disagreements will now end with the loss of Life? It is not uncommon for a run-of-the-mill Domestic Abuse call to end with a dead Wife, a dead Officer, and a Husband who committed Suicide. So please take my opening scripture literally and be Vigilant.

In my extensive research of the scriptures, I have not found any description of the Devil holding a trident: nor having a red-colored complexion, no spade tongue, no fangs, and no long tail. This seems to be a creation of pop culture manifest through old wives' tales, fables, books, and movies. Satan is behind this deception because this serves as part of his unholy purpose. Consider, if you will, who would seek to follow a creature that looked like the horrible images we have created of him? Let me answer that for you, no one. Because he would be a joke, maybe this is why society does not take the Devil seriously. And believe me, Satan is no joke. He is seeking followers, and he knows how to get them. Hint, the lust of the eyes. I have known people to fall in love with someone they described as the most attractive person they have ever seen. But when they look past the beauty, they saw the deception and discover an ugliness, which causes them to curse the day they ever laid eyes upon the person. "And no marvel; for Satan himself is transformed into an angel of light." (2 Corinthians 11:14).

Let us examine the Why. What is Satan's deal, why does he hate us so? There are many answers to this question, and many are based on any and everything, including a loose interpretation of the scriptures. I have heard different sermons state, "God was away from Heaven and His Throne. On that day war broke out in Heaven." In certain communities, this one story is somewhat popular because there are some similarities to this found in the scriptures. "And there was war in heaven: Michael and his angels fought against the dragon; and the dragon fought and his angels," (Revelation 12:7). This theory has a few holes in it; there are several Old and New Testament scriptures that teach us God is omnipresent. "Can any hide himself in secret places that I shall not see him? saith the Lord. Do not I fill heaven and earth? saith the Lord". (Jeremiah 23:24). Simply put, God is so powerful, He does not have to leave Heaven to visit another place. Also, there are two competing theories on Revelation, chapter 12, verse 7. The first theory is this war in heaven happened before the events in the Garden of Eden. The second theory is that this war will take place after the Rapture, and this is the war of Armageddon. In the story I was raised on - Satan was angry with God because God so loved Man. God gave Man a gift that he gave no other creature in all of creation, including the Angels. God made Man in His Image and Likeness and endowed Man with Freewill. Due to the uniqueness of Man's creation, Satan despises him for it.

Many years ago, I came across this twist to the story. Supposedly, Satan was cast out of Heaven because he refused to accept God's new Angelic assignment for him, which was to serve Man. "For he shall give his angels charge over thee, to keep thee in all thy ways. 12 They shall bear thee up in their hands, lest thou dash thy foot against a stone" (Psalms 91:11-12). Satan took this as the ultimate insult. He served God and only God, the Lord of Host, the great I Am, the Creator of the universe. The Man was a lesser being and not deserving of an Angel of his caliber's time. This angered God, and of course you know what happened next. "How art thou fallen from heaven, O Lucifer, son of the morning! how art thou cut down to the ground, which didst weaken the nations! 13 For thou hast said in thine heart, I will ascend into heaven, I will exalt my throne above the stars of God: I will sit also upon the mount of the congregation, in the sides of the north: 14 I will ascend above the heights of the clouds; I will be like the most High. 15 Yet thou shalt be brought down to hell, to the sides of the pit. 16 They that see thee shall narrowly look upon thee, and consider thee, saying, Is this the man that made the earth to tremble, that did shake kingdoms; 17 That made the world as a wilderness, and destroyed the cities thereof; that opened not the house of his prisoners? 19 But thou art cast out of thy grave like an abominable branch, and as the raiment of those that are slain, thrust through with a sword, that go down to the stones of the pit; as a carcass trodden under feet." (Isaiah 14:12-17,19). I believe all of this factors into Satan's overall master plan. If there is no clear and concise story of his origin and no exact consensus on his appearance, Satan can further advance the narrative that he does not exist. A narrative I might remind you that is so successful, most of humanity prescribes to it today.

My Pastor, M.J. Johnson, once told me that when you are faced with a problem in the scriptures or in life, the solution can always be found in red. As all Bible readers know, when you see scriptures written in red, it indicates that Jesus is speaking. Pastor Johnson taught me always to let Jesus have the last word on any subject matter. Let's apply his method here. What did Jesus say about Satan's fall from grace? "And he said unto them, I beheld Satan as lightning fall from heaven." (Luke 10:18). Additional scriptures also support Jesus' statement. "Therefore hell hath enlarged herself, and opened her mouth without measure: and their glory, and their multitude, and their pomp, and he that rejoiceth, shall descend into it." (Isaiah 5:14). Moving forward, what can we conclude? Based on these scriptures, Satan, at some point in time, was present in Heaven and was cast out because of his sinful actions. Also, since Satan's fate will inevitably end in Hell. And, because of his pure disdain for humanity, he desires that Mankind suffers there with him as well. For the purpose of this book, that is all of the Devil's back story we need. We can now develop a Methodology that will identify and remove Satan from our daily lives and remove him from the lives of the people we love. But, believe me when I say this is easier said than done.

Through my many years in the ministry and countless hours devoted to human observation, I have found that casting out the Devil is a monumental and difficult task. Consider, if you will, my assignment; I must prove to people that they are in a battle for their very Souls. What is most difficult is that many are unaware of the War. And, if that was not enough, their adversary Satan is someone, and something that most people do not believe exists. Case in point, recently, I childishly thought the Devil would be exposed. Regaining the infamy that he once had during the Dark Ages as the Architect of despair and the Bane of Human existence. A position that the Devil held until the arrival of the modern age. How could Satan not get the blame for the year 2020? For God's sake people, we faced a Global Plague. Need I remind you, Satan himself has been described as a Plague.

The Plague of 2020 has unfortunately killed millions of people. May God rest their souls. Please refer to the earlier quote of John chapter 10, verse 10a. How are we missing this? After all, Plagues are one of the signs of the coming Apocalypse. The Apocalypse is a foretold battle between Jesus and, guess who, that's right - Satan. But no, the evil entity behind this Plague was a bat and not the cool one from Gotham City. This one was a dinner course bought at an open Wet Market in Wuhan, China. So, much to my disbelief, it seems Satan has dodged this bullet. Surely the Devil would be blamed for the closings of thousands and thousands of our Churches, Temples, and other houses of Worship. Once again, that would be no; the villains behind these shutdowns were overzealous Politicians. Are you kidding me people? If this is a joke, it is not funny; Politicians are to blame, and that's where you're stopping. Billions of people were not allowed to worship Globally and attend Church services, and no one accused Satan. This affected no other Religions as badly as it did Christianity. The very reason is that new members are born into the Islamic faith. However, within Christianity, our new members are Born Again, meaning they have to come and be converted. Ask yourself, how many people do you think came to Christ during the Pandemic while the doors of God's house were closed? With what we know about Satan and how he operates, it is completely illogical not to hold him responsible for the events of 2020. How did we, the Blood Born Children of God, get here? As Children of God, we should be groaning in our spirit and crying out to Jesus. "Who in the days of his flesh, when he had offered up prayers and supplications with strong crying and tears unto him that was able to save him from death, and was heard in that he feared;" (Hebrews 5:7).

The question of how the Faith arrived at such a sad state, brought me to a grim conclusion that I was not prepared to accept. It appears Christians are no longer concerned about Satan or the salvation through Christ that is being denied Humanity. I should not have found this all too surprising, based solely on the fact. I had to censor some of the information I wanted to place within the pages of this Book. The reason being, is the truth hurts.

"But they refused to hearken, and pulled away the shoulder, and stopped their ears, that they should not hear. 12 Yea, they made their hearts as an adamant stone, lest they should hear the law, and the words which the Lord of hosts hath sent in his spirit by the former prophets: therefore came a great wrath from the Lord of hosts:" (Zechariah 7:11-12)

Chapter One

HOW DID WE GET HERE

"For the time will come when they will not endure sound doctrine; but after their own lusts shall they heap to themselves teachers, having itching ears; 4 And they shall turn away their ears from the truth, and shall be turned unto fables." (2 Timothy 4:3-4).

I was invited to Preach at a church one Sunday many years ago. While there, I heard the Pastor of the church, with tears in his eyes, address his loyal Congregation somewhat harshly. Several members were visibly upset. I pondered, were his words sound doctrine? I know this is a blatant accusation, so allow me to provide some backstory. The Pastor recently received a troubling diagnosis from his doctor, and like many, recovery can be a vicious beast of burden. Unfortunately, he blamed this set of circumstances on his congregation. I have learned over the year that discipleship will often lead to flagrant gossip instead of devotion to the Gospel. Both gossip and gospel can ping the pews. Whispers of gossip by the congregation swirled about how the Pastor used the blame game to ease through the struggles of his health crisis. If I am being honest, I found his accusations interesting but also puzzling. In our talks, I often measure the volume of admiration the Pastor had for his congregation with a long stick. I knew the love he had for his church had no bounds. Love suffers long and is kind. I translate this to mean love is often wrapped in harshness and kindness simultaneously when a Pastor speaks. Over the years, as a residual of my time as a Pastor, love often yields an epiphany that pounds my psyche and cultivates my reasoning. My experiences have brought the full scope of that Pastor's statements many years ago into focus. I bread my point-of-view in the common thoughts and basic elemental views of a Pastor's assignment. It is common thinking that we Pastors should abandon our families so that we might minister to your family. And trust me, we do. I believe that most people secretly think a Pastor should walk with their head bowed, sacrifice much, and expect little. And once again, we do. We will pray for people who will not pray for us; we will give our last dime to the Ministry when others do not give their first tenth. And many Pastors will rarely take a sick day or a day off if they have any say in the matter. The Apostle Paul provides us with an excellent example of the internal struggles Church Elders may endure as leaders of God's people. "But if I live in the flesh, this is the fruit of my labour: yet what I shall choose I wot not. 23 For I am in a strait betwixt two, having a desire to depart, and to be with Christ; which is far better: 24 Nevertheless to abide in the flesh is more needful for you." (Philippians 1:22-24). Pastors often wonder why is the greatest assignment a person could ever receive so riddled with conflict, opposition, and, yes, rebellion. After all, God has chosen this person for a Holy purpose. And therein lies the challenge that bruises our consciousness and swirls in a yoke of shifting resistance, the purpose. Arguably born out of The Great Commission, the purpose is to focus primarily on people. And not just any people, God's people. "And he said unto me, Son of man, I send thee to the children of Israel, to a rebellious nation that hath rebelled against me: they and their fathers have transgressed against me, even unto this very day. 4 For they are impudent children and stiffhearted. I do send thee unto them; and thou shalt say unto them, Thus saith the Lord GOD." (Ezekiel 2:3-4). God's people have been misbehaving for a long time. The children of Israel complained about Moses in the wilderness. They placed Jeremiah, a chosen Prophet of God in a pit. And people claiming to be followers of God had the unmitigated gall to stone Stephen for preaching the truth of Jesus Christ. And they dared to stone Stephen while he prayed for their Souls with his dying gasps. Upon close examination of the Holy Bible, there is a multitude of evidence attesting that leading God's people is a very difficult and dangerous assignment. The stress alone can kill you. And having made this observation, I pray to elicit a threefold response for us-the people of God. First, we should treat our leaders with the love and respect they deserve, for their task is indeed tumultuous. Secondly, we are accounted as sheep and we must behave like sheep. And third, sheep have a greater chance of survival when they follow their Shepherd. As a case in point, the Old Testament is filled with scriptures about God's frustration with the Children of Israel as they continued to sin against Him. The scriptures also provide examples of what actions God would employ to correct Israel's bad behavior, and Israel often found God's corrections were a difficult pill to swallow. It is because of these types of scriptures that we have such an immense cloud of witnesses, so much so that this chapter should have had another name. (The joy of resting in Jesus). Wishful thinking. Who other than a chosen shepherd of God would attempt to lead people of this type, people that will push most leaders to a dire end?

As the true followers of Jesus of Nazareth, we should be the envy of all Nations. "And I will make of thee a great nation, and I will bless thee, and make thy name great; and thou shalt be a blessing:" (Genesis 12:2). Please allow me to make an effort to better explain my position. When I consider the biblical accounts of God's Saints, stories that I have read and studied countless numbers of times. It is evident, that we are granted more physical tools than the Saints of ole. With the benefit of these tools and resources, we can better serve our Father God and glorify His kingdom. Let's take a closer look at one of the Saints I mentioned earlier, Stephen. Unlike us, Stephen did not have the benefit of Christianity being the world's largest Religion at the time of his service. He knew not of the notoriety of Jesus Christ being the head of Christianity, or the annals of history recording Jesus as the most influential Man to have ever lived. Stephen and the early Church had nothing but their unwavering faith in God. Through the mighty power of the Holy Spirit, they ultimately converted the Roman Empire by way of their testimonies, their sacrifices, and in some cases their deaths. And I would also remind you this was not an easy task in itself. Romans were extraordinarily brutal in their behavior toward these Christians. They would often kill followers of Christ for sport in the arena. It is believed that the Roman Emperor Nero once burned Christians as lights for one of his garden parties. But those dedicated Christians did not recant or compromise their faith; by all accounts the Romans cruelty strengthened their resolve. "Who shall separate us from the love of Christ? shall tribulation, or distress, or persecution, or famine, or nakedness, or peril, or sword? 36 As it is written, For thy sake we are killed all the day long; we are accounted as sheep for the slaughter." (Romans 8:35-36). Through their faith and courage, Christianity began to grow and make disciples as it advanced throughout the known world.

So, how is it truly possible the modern Church and the Christians that make up its membership, including myself, have become so weak? How have we become so spiritually powerless that a bat brought us to the very brink of despair? We were not attacked by an invading hoard of pagans hell-bent on destroying Christianity; no, not in the least, it was a plague-riddled bat. I am astounded by the tools and resources we have at our disposal in comparison to the early Church. First and foremost, we have the Holy Bible. Stephen and the early Church did not have Bibles.

Followers of Christ now have the absolute Word of God in its entirety, at their fingertips, all sixty-six books. The premise of the Bible is direct, simple, and elegant. The Old Testament consists of thirty-nine books informing readers that a relationship with God at that time was accomplished through the Mosaic Law. The New Testament is composed of twenty-seven books, that teach readers that Jesus Christ, the Son of God, is the only way humanity can ever have a relationship with God the Father. In this day and age, it is absolutely impossible for a Christian not to have access to a Bible; they are everywhere. I have at least twenty Bibles myself, and I consider whether to add to my collection every single day. You can find the Bible online, in libraries, hotel rooms, and hospitals. As I have discovered, there exist several different interpretations, translated into hundreds of languages. There are Bibles written for children. There are Bibles written for men. There are Bibles written for women. There are Devotional Bibles and Study Bibles. I believe possession and the availability of these Bibles is equivalent to Sound Doctrine. Believers cannot truly emerge victorious as followers of Jesus unless we consult the Bible at every turn. Every morning, every night, everyone, male, female, rich, poor, young, and old. "Only be thou strong and very courageous, that thou mayest observe to do according to all the law, which Moses my servant commanded thee: turn not from it to the right hand or to the left, that thou mayest prosper whithersoever thou goest. 8 This book of the law shall not depart out of thy mouth; but thou shalt meditate therein day and night, that thou mayest observe to do according to all that is written therein: for then thou shalt make thy way prosperous, and then thou shalt have good success." (Joshua 1:7-8).

I seek to understand how we got to the place where many will not hear and follow the incredible and sound doctrine of the Messiah. Confirmation of our biblical mission is as follows. Jesus of Nazareth decreed he would not leave his followers defenseless against the wiles of the Devil. Christ informed the Disciples that he would pray to the Father, so that he would send the Comforter. In response to Jesus' prayer, God decided He would dwell within the Believer. God transformed from Emmanuel, God with us, to Sanctification, God within us. "And I will pray the Father, and he shall give you another Comforter, that he may abide with you for ever; 17 Even the Spirit of truth; whom the world cannot receive, because it seeth him not, neither knoweth him: but ye know him; for he dwelleth with you, and shall be in you." (John 14:16-17). Now the indwelling presence of the Holy Spirit, helps lead and guide us, as we traverse this dangerous sinful land.

So, we have the Bible, Jesus, and the Comforter, but do we have wisdom and understanding? I believe the blessing of the indwelling of the Holy Spirit is one of the most misunderstood concepts in the Bible. Most Christians will say they know their body is the temple in which the Holy Spirit lives. However, it is their actions that are in opposition to that fact. "They profess that they know God; but in works they deny him, being abominable, and disobedient, and unto every good work reprobate." (Titus 1:16). Christians must come to the full understanding that the same power which created the Universe resides in us the Children of God. "And the earth was without form, and void; and darkness was upon the face of the deep. And the Spirit of God moved upon the face of the waters. 3 And God said, Let there be light: and there was light." (Genesis 1:2-3). How did we get here? With all of these advantages, why is the Faith and the faithful in such a state of distress? If you remove from history that plague riddled Bat and the ensuing Pandemic, Church membership totals within Christianity still would reflect a downward trajectory. Thousands of families and millions of people have chosen to walk away from the Faith. While others have chosen not to convert to Christianity. I do not have to quote statistic after statistic for you to understand. Take a long critical look at our Country and the lack of Christian Communities which our Nation was once founded upon.

For the first time in our great Country's history, there are more people in America who do not follow Christ than those of us who follow the Lord.

Now, I am somewhat uncomfortable as a Pastor but encouraged as a Christian. I can hear a soft voice saying, "tread lightly, Child of God." While at the same time, as a Preacher, I proceed now to say something somewhat controversial. This information is not trending. This statement has not gone viral; for us boomers, as my daughter refers to me. It has not been featured on the Evening News. My research has led me to believe something else is at work within Christianity, an unforeseen force behind the Faith's current state of affairs. I now believe I have discovered the cause of our declining membership numbers. The Bible tells us that in the last days, there will be an Event within the Faith that serves as one of the signs of the coming Christ. It is my professional and spiritual opinion that we are in the early stages of the Event, known to us, as the Great Falling Away. "Now we beseech you, brethren, by the coming of our Lord Jesus Christ, and by our gathering together unto him, 2 That ye be not soon shaken in mind, or be troubled, neither by spirit, nor by word, nor by letter as from us, as that the day of Christ is at hand. 3 Let no man deceive you by any means: for that day shall not come, except there come a falling away first, and that man of sin be revealed, the son of perdition;" (2 Thessalonians 2:1-3). My mother used to say, "In all of your getting, please get an understanding." Christians and Christianity must have total clarity on this subject matter because it is so vitally important. You must understand, my brothers and sisters, that the physical and spiritual decline we are currently experiencing within our once vibrant Faith shares similar characteristics as the end-time narrative mentioned in 2 Thessalonians. Likewise, there are other scriptures concerning the last days before Christ returns that also support my theory.

However, what I was not expecting to find, was the unfortunate fact that our current calamity seems to be a creature of our design. "This know also, that in the last days perilous times shall come. 2 For men shall be lovers of their own selves, covetous, boasters, proud, blasphemers, disobedient to parents, unthankful, unholy, 3 Without natural affection, trucebreakers, false accusers, incontinent, fierce, despisers of those that are good, 4 Traitors, heady, highminded, lovers of pleasure more than lovers of God; 5 Having a form of godliness, but denying the power thereof: from such turn away. 6 For of this sort are they which creep into houses, and lead captive silly women laden with sins, led away with divers lusts, 7 Ever learning, and never able to come to the knowledge of the truth." (2 Timothy 3:1-7).

Let me explain; I always believed the Great Falling Away would occur after government sanctions were placed on the Church due to our unwavering resolve not to compromise the Word of God. Or at the least, I believed that people would flee Christianity to participate in some new, exciting, less stringent Spiritual movement. Also, I would not have found it shocking to discover that many walked away from the Faith because they lost hope. It never crossed my mind that Christian unrighteousness would be the underlying reason for the falling away. I will use a movie reference to help you better understand my point. We all have seen movies where the main character travels back in time. But, when our time traveling Hero returns to his present day, he discovers something has gone very wrong. Nothing is the same; somehow, everything has changed, and not for the good. Upon further investigation, our inept time traveler discovers he was the cause of the devastation. And like the time traveler, our behavior has damaged the future. We have caused our children and others to say, "if this is what Christianity is, I want no part of it." If we had practiced what we preached and allowed the truth of God's Word to keep us in righteousness, peoples responses would have been different. "Wherefore, my beloved brethren, let every man be swift to hear, slow to speak, slow to wrath: 20 For the wrath of man worketh not the righteousness of God. 21 Wherefore lay apart all filthiness and superfluity of naughtiness, and receive with meekness the engrafted word, which is able to save your souls. 22 But be ye doers of the word, and not hearers only, deceiving your own selves." (James 1:19-22). Only in our righteous state will our family members and others truly seek out righteousness and ask what must we do to be saved. I hope I have made my case clear because it seems we can blame poor Church attendance and fewer Christian converts on ourselves. Which has also ushered in what appears to be the early stages of the Great Falling Away. For it has begun, and much to my chagrin, we are the blame. I understand that the Great Falling Away must occur because it is written in God's Word. But what is not written is that Christians had to be the reason behind its arrival. I do not know how long we have before the floodgates truly open; only God knows. So, what should we do? There is an old saying, "Don't block the Cross." Loosely translated, it questions whether people can see Jesus through you or are you obscuring the message of the Cross. "And shall say, Cast ye up, cast ye up, prepare the way, take up the stumblingblock out of the way of my people." (Isaiah 57:14).

We all bear some responsibility for the present state of Christianity and its decline. I also believe that deep down in your subconscious, you are aware that you have blocked the view of the Cross at some point in your Christian life. Unfortunately, I know I have. "Neither do men light a candle, and put it under a bushel, but on a candlestick; and it giveth light unto all that are in the house. 16 Let your light so shine before men, that they may see your good works, and glorify your Father which is in heaven." (Matthew 5:15-16). As you can see, we have arrived at a critical juncture within our Faith. We must decide which side of the Cross we will stand on, and I know that sounds laughable, but I am deathly serious. As I stated, we are currently experiencing a deficit as it relates to people visiting and joining the Church, and according to the scriptures, there will come a time when people will start leaving the Church in greater numbers. If the Church is going to remain relevant and viable, we Christians must change our Un-Christian-like behavior and rightly prepare ourselves for the coming battle. "If I shut up heaven that there be no rain, or if I command the locusts to devour the land, or if I send pestilence among my people; 14 If my people, which are called by my name, shall humble themselves, and pray, and seek my face, and turn from their wicked ways; then will I hear from heaven, and will forgive their sin, and will heal their land." (2 Chronicles 7:13-14). If Christians will follow God's instructions as presented in 2 Chronicles chapter 7, verse 14, we can plot a course out of the predicament we presently find ourselves. So, let us take a very in-depth look at this scripture and discover how God will deliver us from this darkness into the marvelous light of His Glory. First, we must look at our leadership; our leaders must be accountable. Leadership is where 2 Chronicles chapter 7 begins; we first find Solomon, the King of Israel, praying and supplication before the Lord. "Now when Solomon had made an end of praying, the fire came down from heaven, and consumed the burnt offering and the sacrifices; and the glory of the Lord filled the house." (2 Chronicles 7:1). As followers of Christ, we are at our strongest when we are humble on our knees. Those leading God's people or a religious household must always remember and teach this principle. Never allow yourself to get to a place in life or your ministry where you are too proud to kneel in prayer.

As I stated earlier, I know trials and tribulations can be associated with leading God's people. Also, God has blessed some Pastors to lead congregations that are the size of small cities, which are spread out over multiple diverse communities and locations. With that said, we must remain cognizant of this fact; leading God’s Congregation should never jeopardize the destination of the congregation.

Which is a place where the Church is without stain or blemish, awaiting the return of Jesus Christ. "That he might present it to himself a glorious Church, not having spot, or wrinkle, or any such thing; but that it should be holy and without blemish." (Ephesians 5:27). As Pastors, we need to look no further than Moses, to see an example of a stressful leadership position. He illustrates the price you may pay to lead God's people. God did not allow Moses to cross over the Jordan river into the Promise Land because of a lapse in judgment as he led the Children of Israel through the wilderness. "And the Lord said unto him, This is the land which I sware unto Abraham, unto Isaac, and unto Jacob, saying, I will give it unto thy seed: I have caused thee to see it with thine eyes, but thou shalt not go over thither. 5 So Moses the servant of the Lord died there in the land of Moab, according to the word of the Lord." (Deuteronomy 34:4-5).

I fully understand the task we have before us as leaders. Many of us have studied and taught the Bible for many years, and we still have only just scratched the surface. There is so much knowledge and information a Pastor must disseminate to those that he is assigned to shepherd. It is not unusual for it to feel overwhelming at times. And because of this monumental task, some leaders have chosen to take shortcuts by watering down and cherry-picking from the scriptures what they deem suitable for their congregations. When we choose not to convey God's true message to His Children because we deem it to be a hard truth. Or outside influences believe it be an unpopular subject matter, we do a disservice to God, ourselves, and those we have been called to lead. This type of behavior has shown itself to be detrimental to the body of Christ time and time again. "And unto the angel of the church in Sardis write; These things saith he that hath the seven Spirits of God, and the seven stars; I know thy works, that thou hast a name that thou livest, and art dead. 2 Be watchful, and strengthen the things which remain, that are ready to die: for I have not found thy works perfect before God. 3

Remember therefore how thou hast received and heard, and hold fast, and repent. If therefore thou shalt not watch, I will come on thee as a thief, and thou shalt not know what hour I will come upon thee." (Revelation 3:1-3). It is our assignment as Shepherds of God's flock to preach and teach the Word in its entirety. If we do not, we leave ourselves and others vulnerable to the attacks of Satan. "My people are destroyed for lack of knowledge: because thou hast rejected knowledge, I will also reject thee, that thou shalt be no priest to me: seeing thou hast forgotten the law of thy God, I will also forget thy children." (Hosea 4:6).

Transitioning from the leaders to those of us being led, 2 Chronicles chapter 7 verse 14 opens with a statement to God's people. I do not care what denomination you are, whether you worship on a Saturday or Sunday. When you worship, I do not care if it is a Church, a Hall, or a Temple. We must move past these things that separate us in the Body of Christ. The only important issue is the Relationship; that is all we need to concern ourselves with. Are you in a true relationship with the Father? And if you love the Father, then you must love me and not only me but all of God's Children, sinner and saint alike. "If a man say, I love God, and hateth his brother, he is a liar: for he that loveth not his brother whom he hath seen, how can he love God whom he hath not seen? 21 And this commandment have we from him, That he who loveth God love his brother also." (1 John 4:20-21).

Our next step is humility. A humble spirit is powerful because it is of God, it can lift us and others out of despair, which is sorely needed. "Humble yourselves in the sight of the Lord, and he shall lift you up." (James 4:10) One thing that the world and the worldly are not is humble, for they are ruled by their pride, which leads to destruction.

Next is prayer; I cannot stress this enough, prayer is vital if you are a Child of God seeking to build and keep His Kingdom. Pray that God's Will is done on Earth as in Heaven. Pray in the morning before work or school, pray throughout the day, pray at the end of your day, pray, pray, and pray yet again. "And he spake a parable unto them to this end, that men ought always to pray, and not to faint;" (Luke 18:1).

After prayer in 2nd Chronicles chapter 7 verse 14, God tells us to seek His face. How do we accomplish this? After all, God is a Spirit and does not have a physical face. In Hebrew, the face can be translated to presence, so God our Father tells His Children to seek His presence. "And ye shall seek me, and find me, when ye shall search for me with all your heart." (Jeremiah 29:13). Let us examine our hearts as Children of God. What are we actively searching for? Is it God, or is it something or someone else? Only you and God truly know the answer to this question. Now, what if we took the term face literally? What do you spend most of your time gazing upon? Is it the Bible or Christian television? How about the countless Sermons and church services found on the internet? "I will lift up mine eyes unto the hills, from whence cometh my help. 2 My help cometh from the Lord, which made heaven and earth." (Psalm 121:1-2). Or are we constantly staring into the eyes of the unrighteous and unrighteousness? "Hell and destruction are never full; so the eyes of man are never satisfied." (Proverbs 27:20). I know in many cases that we feel it's just harmless entertainment, but is it? What we now see on television has become our reality. The sex, violence, profanity, and obscenities we look upon are now so commonplace that they have become the norm in our society. And trust me, dear readers, long-term exposure to this type of sin will begin to contaminate your very Soul. Also, with the advent of the world wide web, we can now view the pain, suffering, misfortunes, and in some cases, the very death of our fellow man live and in real-time. Through whistle-blowers and congressional investigations. It has recently come to light that the creators of many of the internet platforms hosting content viewed by us were designed to be addictive. These websites were created to keep users on their sites for hours. Please be aware that there is an unholy science to the design of their Algorithms. Satan and the Developers of these websites know the average human mind can only entertain one thought at a time. He knows the more time you spend looking at worldly things, the less time you spend looking at Holy things, such as the Bible and Jesus.

Take the Apostle Peter for an example. As long as Peter kept his eyes on Jesus, he could accomplish the supernatural. But the very moment Peter took his eyes off of Jesus and looked at the natural, he started to think about the natural and began to drown. "And straightway Jesus constrained his disciples to get into a ship, and to go before him unto the other side, while he sent the multitude away. 24 But the ship was now in the midst of the sea, tossed with waves: for the wind was contrary. 25 And in the fourth watch of the night Jesus went unto them, walking on the sea. 26 And when the disciples saw him walking on the sea, they were troubled, saying, It is a spirit; and they cried out for fear. 27 But straightway Jesus spake unto them, saying, Be of good cheer; it is I; be not afraid. 28 And Peter answered him and said, Lord, if it be thou, bid me come unto thee on the water. 29 And he said, Come. And when Peter was come down out of the ship, he walked on the water, to go to Jesus. 30 But when he saw the wind boisterous, he was afraid; and beginning to sink, he cried, saying, Lord, save me. 31 And immediately Jesus stretched forth his hand, and caught him, and said unto him, O thou of little faith, wherefore didst thou doubt?" (Matthew 14:22,24-31). This is what Satan desires; he wants you distracted. So much so; you have little time for the Bible or God, which, as we know, can have deadly consequences. Brothers and sisters, ask yourself, would Jesus find these websites entertaining? The answer is a simple resounding no; Jesus would not. So, how could you or any other Child of God find this evil entertaining? "Let thine eyes look right on, and let thine eyelids look straight before thee." (Proverbs 4:25).

Next, in 2 Chronicles chapter 7 verse 14, God asks us to turn from our wicked ways. This can be tough because we know and have seen wickedness and wicked people, and we consider ourselves not wicked. In our minds, wickedness is reserved for the ungodly heathens. You are right. We are not heathens, and God never said we were wicked. However, God did say we have wicked ways. I will not frighten you with a long-drawn-out list of our wicked ways, but I will provide you with the categories in which they belong. Complacency - "And I will say to my soul, Soul, thou hast much goods laid up for many years; take thine ease, eat, drink, and be merry." (Luke 12:19). Apathy - "I know thy works, that thou art neither cold nor hot: I would thou wert cold or hot. 16 So then because thou art lukewarm, and neither cold nor hot, I will spue thee out of my mouth." (Revelation 3:15-16). Compromise - "Therefore, my beloved brethren, be ye stedfast, unmoveable, always abounding in the work of the Lord, forasmuch as ye know that your labour is not in vain in the Lord." (1 Corinthians 15:58). There you have it my fellow Christians: our Achilles heel, **Complacency**, **Apathy**, and **Compromise**, three big words for sin. "Therefore to him that knoweth to do good, and doeth it not, to him it is sin." (James 4:17).

The final thing we must do, as stated in 2 Chronicles chapter 7 verse 14, is wait on the Lord and receive our blessing. God must and will honor His Word, if we have accomplished these requirements in Spirit and Truth. "So shall my word be that goeth forth out of my mouth: it shall not return unto me void, but it shall accomplish that which I please, and it shall prosper in the thing whereto I sent it." (Isaiah 55:11).

There you have it, my thoughts on how we got here. Hopefully, now that you know where we are and what's to come, you will prepare yourself to fight the good fight of faith. So, turn the page and let us begin.

"Fight the good fight of faith, lay hold on eternal life, whereunto thou art also called, and hast professed a good profession before many witnesses." (1 Timothy 6:12).

Chapter Two

THE FIGHT BEGINS

"And he said, Hearken ye, all Judah, and ye inhabitants of Jerusalem, and thou king Jehoshaphat, Thus saith the Lord unto you, Be not afraid nor dismayed by reason of this great multitude; for the battle is not yours, but God's." (2 Chronicles 20:15).

Most would view this chapter's title as a metaphor for their daily struggles. If they did, they would be completely wrong. "The Fight Begins" is a literary warning shot leading to imminent death, meant to be taken quite literally. The battle is lost unless we understand our destiny and what it takes to possess the land. The Bible is a detailed chronicle and prophecy of hundreds of vicious fights with a grueling and murderous adversary operating inside a spiritual inception and a physical realm. As I stated earlier in the Introduction, most people are not aware that they are in a grueling, grinding, psychotic battle with humanity's greatest adversary-commonly known as the Devil. Many people face this vicious threat disguised as a series of unfortunate and unavoidable challenges. It's ups and downs, good and bad - never balling up their spiritual fist to break the lock and hold of Satan. Satan slowly grabs at our spiritual souls throughout our lifetime, hoping to crush us. If the average man has a good day, they chalk it up to being lucky. On the other hand, if they have a bad day, they say, "you can't win them all." What's truly frightening is that most people don't realize every day is a bad day. Every minute of every hour of every single new day. Brings each man, woman, and child on this planet closer to an afterlife spent in the eternal flames of what the Bible commonly refers to as Hell. Without a personal relationship with our Lord and Savior, Jesus Christ, suffering will be an unfortunate end for us all. "Behold, I was shapen in iniquity, and in sin did my mother conceive me." (Psalm 51:5). Life is a crescendo of punishments bestowed on humanity for the original sin of our forefathers, Adam and Eve. How can we describe this original sin? "Wherefore, as by one man sin entered into the world, and death by sin; and so death passed upon all men, for that all have sinned:" (Romans 5:12). The biblical definition of original sin has a deadly after-effect that has lasted throughout time.

I hear you - my secular brothers and sisters whispering under your breath, "that is a steep price to pay for just eating an apple." However, they disobeyed the Creator, the most loving, omnipotent being and the Universe. Who said to Adam and Eve, "do not eat of this tree." "Do not eat of this tree" is the first of seven affirmations to remember, repeat, and fortify us in our fight. If Adam and Eve had eaten just a plain ole apple, we would not have inherited this poisonous plague that has sickened and destroyed countless generations. The apple, as a representation of the fruit that grew on the Tree of Knowledge, is a concoction of Man's imagination. The real fruit and the Tree of Knowledge have not been seen in the earthly realm by man since Adam and Eve ate of it. I understand how some may misconstrue God as an endless bastion of mercy for any of Man's offenses, and disregard His own truth's consequences on our lives. "For his merciful kindness is great toward us: and the truth of the Lord endureth for ever. Praise ye the Lord." (Psalm 117:2). As this scripture alludes to, God does have the capacity to show mercy and forgive those who have offended Him. But this was not a minor offense;

they set in motion an evil that attacked the very foundation of Creation. Ineptly unleashing death and destruction, as well as a never-ending struggle between good and evil. Along with an evolving wickedness of betrayal and deceit, the promise of toil and pain, and anger of our Father, the Lord God Almighty. Not only did they offend the Creator, but they also offended every one of us! There could be no mercy for Adam, considering he violated the first and only command ever given him at that time. "And the Lord God commanded the man, saying, Of every tree of the garden thou mayest freely eat: 17 But of the tree of the knowledge of good and evil, thou shalt not eat of it: for in the day that thou eatest thereof thou shalt surely die." (Genesis 2:16-17). Adam and Eve decided to listen to Satan and not God. Circle your wagons around that for a second. Our forefathers, by default, aligned themselves with Satan. Like many of us, who follow or lean to our own understanding. Eve hearkened to Satan and was downgraded from her original spiritual brilliance and dominance to feeling naked and covering herself in fear. Could they have possibly comprehended the untold cost of their desire to educate themselves in the knowledge of good and evil? Do most not conform to the thought that good or bad knowledge is power? Is this not how people think today? In the beginning, God may have wanted good without evil for us, but knowledge can be a wicked mistress.

This is the second of seven affirmations to remember, repeat, and fortify us in our fight. Their offense had much larger implications. In choosing to believe Satan, they chose not to believe God. Subsequently, their actions meant God had lied to them. "God is not a man, that he should lie; neither the son of man, that he should repent: hath he said, and shall he not do it? or hath he spoken, and shall he not make it good?" (Numbers 23:19). Unbeknownst to Adam and Eve their spiritual failure is seen by the meager mind of Man as a dilemma for God.

Why did Adam and Eve make this terrible decision? One school of thought states, "Man is inherently evil." And I will admit that Man's behavior provides mountains of evidence to support this theory. But, if you accept this logic, it would make the Bible fictitious. The Bible states that Man was created in the image and likeness of God. "And God said, Let us make man in our image, after our likeness: and let them have dominion over the fish of the sea, and over the fowl of the air, and over the cattle, and over all the earth, and over every creeping thing that creepeth upon the earth. 27 So God created man in his own image, in the image of God created he him; male and female created he them." (Genesis 1:26-27). One thing all Christians can agree upon, regardless of how they interpret the scriptures, is, that God is good. "And Jesus said unto him, Why callest thou me good? there is none good but one, that is, God." (Mark 10:18). Since God is good, and Man was created in His likeness and image, then by default, Man's original sinless state was also good. This is the third of seven affirmations to remember, repeat, and fortify us in our fight.

That goodness may have played a major role in Adam and Eve's downfall. I think we can all agree due to the uniqueness of Adam and Eve's creation, they were unlike any other humans that ever lived or walked the face of this Earth. They were devoid of hate: anger, strife, greed, jealousy, envy, or any aspect of sin whatsoever. Not only were they created absent sin, but they also had no idea of what sin was. They could not speak it; they could not find it, they could not comprehend it. Sin did not exist in their world. Not only were they created good, but everything around them was also good. "And God saw every thing that he had made, and, behold, it was very good. And the evening and the morning were the sixth day." (Genesis 1:31). My conclusion is this, Adam and Eve had no idea Satan was lying to them. They were the original goody-two-shoes. They did not possess the **Knowledge** that was necessary for them to ascertain what a lie was. Need I remind you of the name of the tree in which they ate of?

It was called the Tree of **Knowledge**. My grandmother always said, "If it sounds too good to be true, then it probably is not true." Adam and Eve could not hearken unto my grandmother's wisdom because all they knew was truth. Every word ever spoken to them before they converse with Satan the snake was true. God had only exposed them to the truth of His Word. The words spoken by Satan on that unfortunate day were literally the first lies ever told to Man. So, I conclude that Man was not created inherently evil. However, he was incredibly naive. This is the fourth of seven affirmations to remember, repeat, and fortify us in our fight.

Of course, this may not be a popular sentiment with my own counterparts within the theological community. "Reverend Woods, are you seriously suggesting that Original Sin, the very sin that condemned all of humanity to death and an eternity spent possibly in Hell's fire, was due to Adam and Eve being gullible?". Yes, you are correct. That's exactly what I am suggesting. They were extremely gullible. It is my opinion in this case, and at that time, Adam and Eve were truly babes in the woods. I also believe this is why God issued them a punishment instead of a curse. Man's punishment was not as severe as the curse placed upon the serpent. "And the Lord God said unto the serpent, Because thou hast done this, thou art cursed above all cattle, and above every beast of the field; upon thy belly shalt thou go, and dust shalt thou eat all the days of thy life:" (Genesis 3:14). I arrived at this understanding when I consider their behavior after they had eaten from the Tree of Knowledge. "And they heard the voice of the Lord God walking in the garden in the cool of the day: and Adam and his wife hid themselves from the presence of the Lord God amongst the trees of the garden. 9 And the Lord God called unto Adam, and said unto him, Where art thou? 10 And he said, I heard thy voice in the garden, and I was afraid, because I was naked; and I hid myself. 11 And he said, Who told thee that thou wast naked? Hast thou eaten of the tree, whereof I commanded thee that thou shouldest not eat? 12 And the man said, The woman whom thou gavest to be with me, she gave me of the tree, and I did eat. 13 And the Lord God said unto the woman, What is this that thou hast done? And the woman said, The serpent beguiled me, and I did eat." (Genesis 3:8-13). Man has just committed the world's greatest sin, and the best excuse they could concoct is the blame game. At least the serpent shows he took some personal responsibility by not offering a lame reason for his sinful actions. Satan is the king of deceit and the master of lies. "An heart that deviseth wicked imaginations, feet that be swift in running to mischief, 19 A false witness that speaketh lies, and he that soweth discord among brethren." (Proverbs 6:18-19).

I have been scammed once or twice in my lifetime. In other words, I am prepared to fight Satan on many fronts because I know his dirty tactics. The Bible's strongest man, Samson, was brought to his knees by Satan's lies. Also David, a man who loved God beyond measure, succumbed to the trickery and deceit of Satan "And when he had removed him, he raised up unto them David to be their king; to whom also he gave their testimony, and said, I have found David the son of Jesse, a man after mine own heart, which shall fulfill all my will." (Acts 13:22).

I hope I have clarified my position. Adam and Eve were simply outmatched by the Devil. What we see here is not an overlooked design flaw or ghost in the machine; it is only the challenges of God being a true Father to Man. Loosely put, as all parents have discovered, children have a mind of their own. God had and has the same problem with His children as we have with ours. They just won't listen. Case in point, I have a close friend who made plans for his daughter to attend one of the many colleges to which she was accepted. She, on the other hand, wanted to marry her high school sweetheart and start a family. Guess which route she chose? Here is a hint, my friend now is the reluctantly proud grandfather of three wonderful and loving grandchildren, unfortunately from a divorced daughter.

If this example or any other I have mentioned possibly strikes a chord with you, then the fight I referenced at the beginning should be coming into focus now. Life is truly a fight, even in folly, fancy, and fun. Becoming followers of Jesus Christ does not promise a life of reclining on flower beds of ease. We must constantly stay on guard, watching and waiting for the next attack from Satan. My grandfather used to say, "If you are not in a storm, then you have just come out of a storm. And if you have not just come out of a storm, look down the road at those dark clouds and smell the rain in the air. A storm is coming." Brothers and sisters, I tell you the truth. If you have a spouse, a storm is coming. If you have children, a storm is coming. And, if you love the Lord, a storm is most certainly coming.

Now let us return to the dilemma for God that I referred to earlier. First, let me state that my usage of the term dilemma is not used here as an example of a problem for God. We know God is omnipotent or all-powerful; in other words, He does not have problems. I only chose the term dilemma to help with our feeble comprehension. "Ah Lord God! behold, thou hast made the heaven and the earth by thy great power and stretched out arm, and there is nothing too hard for thee:" (Jeremiah 32:17). The delay in the original plan is the Dilemma. This is the fifth of seven affirmations to remember, repeat, and fortify us in our fight. The Bible provides details of God's original plan for Man before he sinned. What would the life of an eternal, sinless Man be? "What is man, that thou art mindful of him? and the son of man, that thou visitest him? 5 For thou hast made him a little lower than the angels, and hast crowned him with glory and honour. 6 Thou madest him to have dominion over the the works of thy hands; thou hast put all things under his feet:" (Psalm 8:4-6). As described here, Man was assigned caretaker of the Earth. God created a Heaven on Earth for him; it was paradise. It does not require any stretch of the imagination to see the current state of the Earth is not a paradise. It is quite evident that this was not God's original vision for Man or the Earth. "And it repented the Lord that he had made man on the earth, and it grieved him at his heart." (Genesis 6:6). Just as the first book in the Bible, Genesis, provides us answer to the question of why was Man created. We can also use the last book of the Bible, Revelation, to solidify that point. "Thou art worthy, O Lord, to receive glory and honour and power: for thou hast created all things, and for thy pleasure they are and were created." (Revelation 4:11). In conjunction, the last chapters of Revelation-it's prophecies-yield further insight into what God had envisioned for the Earth, and Man. The prophecies concerning the end of days prove God has no use for this sinful Earth or its contents. "And I saw a new heaven and a new earth: for the first heaven and the first earth were passed away; and there was no more sea. 2 And I John saw the holy city, new Jerusalem, coming down from God out of heaven, prepared as a bride adorned for her husband. 3 And I heard a great voice out of heaven saying, Behold, the tabernacle of God is with men, and he will dwell with them, and they shall be his people, and God himself shall be with them, and be their God. 4 And God shall wipe away all tears from their eyes; and there shall be no more death, neither sorrow, nor crying, neither shall there be any more pain: for the former things are passed away." (Revelation 21:1-4).

Hopefully, now you understand why we fight. We see God again physically fellowship with Man here on Earth, which he did in the beginning. We also learn Man is no longer plagued by pain, suffering, and sorrow, and most importantly, by death. This is what God truly wanted, or what His Will was for Man since the beginning. This is the sixth of seven affirmations to remember, repeat, and fortify us in our fight. This scripture indicates at some point; God will allow Man to drink from the fountain from which living water flows. "And he said unto me, it is done. I am Alpha and Omega, the beginning and the end. I will give unto him that is athirst of the fountain of the water of life freely." (Revelation 21:6). Or Man was granted permission to eat from the Tree of Life. "In the midst of the street of it, and on either side of the river, was there the tree of life, which bare twelve manner of fruits, and yielded her fruit every month: and the leaves of the tree were for the healing of the nations." (Revelation 22:2).

Revelation shows us Man will gain at the end of time what he originally lost at the beginning of time. This brings me to an interesting point: if we are given at the end what we once possessed at the beginning before Man sinned. It stands to reason that at some point in the beginning, God would have allowed Adam and Eve to eat from the Tree of Knowledge. The reasoning for my last inclination is more complex than a simple yes or no. There are two schools of thought on this matter. The first group is of the opinion that God would have never allowed Man to eat the fruit from the Tree of Knowledge. This group believes Man would become god-like and thus the same as God, and the Almighty could not abide that reality. "And the Lord God said, Behold, the man is become as one of us, to know good and evil: and now, lest he put forth his hand, and take also of the tree of life, and eat, and live for ever." (Genesis 3:22). The ideology behind their belief is, God is a jealous God and Man elevated to an equal position would anger God. "Thou shalt have no other gods before me." (Exodus 20:3). The second group is of the opinion that God would have eventually allowed man to eat from the Tree of Knowledge. This group believes the answer can also be found in both the last and first books of the Bible. I am a member of this particular group and believe it to be God's Will.

I would ask the reader to pay close attention moving forward because the following stories and examples have complicated injections, inferences, and subtleties. Christians know God's Will and Words are absolute. "Hast thou not known? hast thou not heard, that the everlasting God, the Lord, the Creator of the ends of the earth, fainteth not, neither is weary? there is no searching of his understanding." (Isaiah 40:28). In layman's terms; what God wants to happen, will happen because He has the power to make it happen, and if He speaks a word, it will come to pass. "The grass withereth, the flower fadeth: but the word of our God shall stand for ever." (Isaiah 40:8). Let's use one of the Apostle Paul's most problematic missionary journeys as an example of the Will of God. God Willed, or as we say, wanted Paul to preach in Rome. "After these things were ended, Paul purposed in the spirit, when he had passed through Macedonia and Achaia, to go to Jerusalem, saying, After I have been there, I must also see Rome." (Acts 19:21). And despite being shipwrecked on the way there and also bitten by a poisonous snake. Paul kept the faith because he knew God's will would be done. "And now I exhort you to be of good cheer: for there shall be no loss of any man's life among you, but of the ship. 23 For there stood by me this night the angel of God, whose I am, and whom I serve, 24 Saying, Fear not, Paul; thou must be brought before Caesar: and, lo, God hath given thee all them that sail with thee. 25 Wherefore, sirs, be of good cheer: for I believe God, that it shall be even as it was told me." (Acts 27:22-25).

As exemplified, if it is the Will of God, Satan will do his damnedest to prevent you from achieving success. "And when Paul had gathered a bundle of sticks, and laid them on the fire, there came a viper out of the heat, and fastened on his hand. 5 And he shook off the beast into the fire, and felt no harm." (Acts 28:3,5). In defiance of Satan and the journeys many problems, Paul did preach in Rome. "And we came to Rome, the centurion delivered the prisoners to the captain of the guard: but Paul was suffered to dwell by himself with a soldier that kept him. 30 And Paul dwelt two whole years in his own hired house, and received all that came in unto him, 31 Preaching the kingdom of God, and teaching those things which concern the Lord Jesus Christ, with all confidence, no man forbidding him." (Acts 28:16,30-31).

As we have seen by these scriptures, no power in heaven or hell can stop the Word of God and the Will of God.

Now here is my point. Those that are blessed to dwell with God in Revelation chapter 21, verse 3, have been saved by Christ through faith. This means they suffered under Adam's curse and thus had full knowledge of good and evil. But, being redeemed from the curse by the blood of Christ Jesus, they suffer not the final payment of the curse, which was an eternity spent in Hell's Fire. So, if the final state of a redeemed Man is one of eternal life and **Knowledge of good and evil**, then it stands to reason that the original state of a sinless Adam would have been the same. In conclusion, it appears Adam and Eve jumped the gun and received from Satan what God would have eventually given them in His own due time. This is the seventh of seven affirmations to remember, repeat, and fortify us in our fight. And I might add, without any strings attached.

This serves as an excellent transition for my final point in this chapter. If we are going to experience success and win this fight; fighting the Adam and Eve Syndrome. We must learn how to wait on the Lord. "Wait on the Lord: be of good courage, and he shall strengthen thine heart: wait, I say, on the Lord." (Psalm 27:14). The Bible contains, by my rough estimate, over several thousand promises. And to put it plainly, those promises say someone or something will be blessed, or someone or something will be cursed. As followers of Jesus Christ, we must hold to God's promises and do as Paul did in my earlier example: stand by faith on God's Word. Always hold to this fact, a blessing delayed is not a blessing denied.

Let us consider King David as the ideal example. Bible Scholars put David at or around the age of fifteen when the Prophet Samuel anointed him to be the future King of Israel. "And the Lord said unto Samuel, How long wilt thou mourn for Saul, seeing I have rejected him from reigning over Israel? fill thine horn with oil, and go, I will send thee to Jesse the Bethlehemite: for I have provided me a king among his sons. 13 Then Samuel took the horn of oil, and anointed him in the midst of his brethren: and the Spirit of the Lord came upon David from that day forward. So Samuel rose up, and went to Ramah." (1 Samuel 16:1,13). But, David never ruled as a young teen. Many obstacles, trials, and tribulations would befall David before he would sit on the throne. "David was thirty years old when he began to reign, and reigned forty years." (2 Samuel 5:4). As it relates to God, patience is truly a virtue. He moves in His own time. Furthermore, other believers and I have discovered that while you are waiting on the Lord, a person usually grows in wisdom and matures in faith. This also helps the person fortify himself for the fight to come. Just as it is with a blessing, the same holds for prayer because a prayer not answered is not necessarily a prayer not heard.

There are many reasons why the answer to your prayers may not be forthcoming. In the book of Daniel, the scriptures state that Daniel prayed to God for guidance as it related to the Children of Israel. God heard Daniel's prayers and sent an angel with the answer, but an evil entity or angel delayed the angel of God for twenty-one days. "Then said he unto me, Fear not, Daniel: for from the first day that thou didst set thine heart to understand, and to chasten thyself before thy God, thy words were heard, and I am come for thy words. 13 But the prince of the kingdom of Persia withstood me one and twenty days: but, lo, Michael, one of the chief princes, came to help me; and I remained there with the kings of Persia. 14 Now I am come to make thee understand what shall befall thy people in the latter days: for yet the vision is for many days." (Daniel 10:12-14).

There you have it, my brothers and sisters. We are at War, but through these seven affirmations and a dose of patience, you can understand the war and empower your spirit during this time of trouble. We have discovered that the first battle started at the very beginning of time. And, it would not surprise me if this War were to end while we lived. But, if it does not, we must continue to stand and fight.

"For though we walk in the flesh, we do not war after the flesh:" (2 Corinthians 10:3).

Chapter Three

COLLATERAL DAMAGE

"The Lord is longsuffering, and of great mercy, forgiving iniquity and transgression, and by no means clearing the guilty, visiting the iniquity of the fathers upon the children unto the third and fourth generation." (Numbers 14:18).

There is a term the military use when a particular operation has suffered some unforeseen incident. This term relays information to those that have a need-to-know that there arose complications despite a well-executed plan for an intended target. The term is called Collateral Damage. It covers the whole kit and caboodle - anything from the loss of life to an unforeseen injury, equipment loss, and personal property damage. Most of us have become familiar with the term because we have heard it used in movies or on television. One of the reasons we remember this term is because it is so easily understood. It stains our memories. We have observed collateral damage many times in our own lives. For example, my son once threw a ball at his big sister; the ball accidentally knocked her cell phone out of her hand, scratching it. The unfortunate mishap with the phone was collateral damage. My daughter was upset with her brother, but she knew there was no malice in his actions, so she soon forgave him. Fortunately, my son's antics ended with a smile on my daughter's face. But if there is anything most of us have learned from life, is, that few experiences have a happy ending. The boy does not always get the girl. The frog is not a prince, and papa does not always save the family farm.

In my capacity as a Minister, I have counseled individuals and couples experiencing rough patches in their relationships. I have observed firsthand the devastating effects of one careless act of sin. And the untold amount of collateral damage visited upon these individuals and their relationships. The stories I am about to share with you are not the private and personal details of anyone I have counseled or been acquainted with through my professional career in the Clergy. They are an amalgamation of the many stories I have heard over a lifetime of human interaction and observation. I believe that each story will, in itself, provide us an ideal example of collateral damage. I also believe these examples will give greater insight into the tactics of Satan. Can you imagine the joy stolen from a couple when a doctor informs them the wife is pregnant with their first child? However, test results have also shown the wife has contracted a case of Herpes since her last visit seven months earlier. The husband never could have imagined this would be the end result of a one-night stand he had months ago with a colleague at an out-of-town business conference. Satan has turned what should have been one of the most joyous events in this young couple's life into a living nightmare. One that threatens the wife, the husband, and their unborn child's health. If that was not punishment enough for the young husband, he is now left to wonder if his marriage will survive this regrettable betrayal. God only knows. Here is another scenario. It is the first day of class at one of our nation's largest universities, but there seems to be an empty seat in freshman economics. The student that is supposed to occupy the seat is at a clinic on the other side of town awaiting a medical procedure. Little did the naive small-town girl know; that a weekend visit to the college and sneaking away to a wild frat party off campus would send her to an abortion clinic nine weeks later.

Worst yet, this is just the beginning of her sorrows. There will arise complications after the procedure, and she is told that she will never be able to have children.

These are just a few examples of collateral damage. I have personally seen churches destroyed over the Pastor's sins. I have also observed the loss of a business that has been under family control for decades. And what is truly disturbing - the business survived economic turmoil and the loss of its founder. But it could not survive the act of one family member's interaction with Satan. We all saw the damage that befell the innocent victims of Bernie Madoff. Let us consider the collateral damage Israel suffered because of King David. As you may or may not have known, David is one of the most fascinating characters in the Bible. And because his story is present in both the Old and New Testament scriptures, we will examine David in this chapter and others. The Bible tells us that God punished Israel because David sinned. "And Satan stood up against Israel, and provoked David to number Israel. 14 So the Lord sent pestilence upon Israel: and there fell of Israel seventy thousand men. 17 And David said unto God, Is it not I that commanded the people to be numbered? even I it is that have sinned and done evil indeed; but as for these sheep, what have they done? let thine hand, I pray thee, O Lord my God, be on me, and on my father's house; but not on thy people, that they should be plagued." (1 Chronicles 21:1,14,17).

The divorce rate among Christians today is roughly the same as in the secular community. The disgruntled parents of the sixties and seventies never considered that their decision to divorce would bring about what some believe is the beginning of the end of marriage as we know it in America today. Divorce is single-handedly one of the most destructive statutes on the books to date. I have observed its ruinous effects on friends, families, and communities. Occasionally, a Christian acquaintance will ask my advice on how they can end their marriage and not jeopardize their relationship with God. I usually put forth this question, do you believe God is all-powerful? Without pause or hesitation, everyone answers yes to this question. It is a no-brainer; sinners and saints know God is all-powerful. My next question, however, is not usually answered so quickly. When they do answer, it is not in the affirmative. That question is, do you believe God has the power to save your marriage? Unfortunately, after I have put forth this question, I have observed that most Christians are not willing or able to put faith in God's power to save their marriage. If you find this statement troubling, it is only because the truth hurts. Many Christians abandoned their marriages because of their own selfish reasons, and they need no help from God to do this. We, as believers, are often confronted with problems in life that we decide to handle on our own without any assistance from God. Our actions are saying to God thanks but no thanks. I got this, and I don't need your help. This lack of faith within the Body of Christ is unfathomable. I had no plans to discuss faith in any detail within this book. I feel it is such a massive undertaking, and it deserves more time and research than I am prepared to give at this point. But not to worry; I am currently in prayer and supplication, and hopefully, God will allow me to make Faith the subject of my next book.

What I will say now about faith will be considered somewhat controversial by the Christian community. I can state it here in this chapter, just as well as in any of the other chapters. The lack of faith is the underlying cause of so many problems within Christianity, and the unfortunate results of those problems are collateral damage. Now here is where the controversy comes into play within my narrative. I have no doubt that most Christians know what faith is. However, what I have witnessed over decades spent within the Christian Community, is only a minimal amount of us live by faith. The sheer magnitude or size of Christians who lack faith within the Body of Christ runs the gamut from Pastors to Parishioners. Part of the problem is most of us have become so conformed to the world that it is difficult, if not impossible, for us to die to this world and live spiritually. "If ye then be risen with Christ, seek those things which are above, where Christ sitteth on the right hand of God. 2 Set your affection on things above, not on things on the earth. 3 For ye are dead, and your life is hid with Christ in God. (Colossians 3:1-3). We have been so conditioned by the world and its systems that we put more faith in them than God and His Word. We live by the mantra that there is nothing free in life. If you want to get ahead in this life, you have to work your fingers to the bone, and if that does not work, beg, borrow, or steal. This is not a new problem with the Children of God. Jesus was also troubled by the absence or lack of faith within the Children of Israel. "When Jesus heard these things, he marvelled at him, and turned him about, and said unto the people that followed him, I say unto you, I have not found so great faith, no, not in Israel." (Luke 7:9). I am not going to ask you to check off a list of items to determine if you walk by faith (e.g., giving, studying, and love). What I will request of you, is to ask God if He is pleased with your faith walk. Please, be truly honest with yourself. The fate of Christianity and your soul may depend on it.

Now, back to collateral damage. Satan is not all-knowing, but he is experienced in human behavior. He has destroyed countless numbers of families and harvested millions of souls through his use of collateral damage. Satan utterly relies on it; what I find frightening is that it is somewhat simple in its application. Satan's belief is, why settle for one soul when you can take two or more. As I have shown in the past pages, Satan has been plotting against Man from the beginning. He is cunning and patient; he plays the long game. "Now the serpent was more subtil than any beast of the field which the Lord God had made. And he said unto the woman, Yea, hath God said, Ye shall not eat of every tree of the garden?" (Genesis 3:1). Notice the clear recognizable hook there. Satan puts forward a question to Eve, that he already knew the answer to. "And the serpent said unto the woman, Ye shall not surely die: 5 For God doth know that in the day ye eat thereof, then your eyes shall be opened, and ye shall be as gods, knowing good and evil." (Genesis 3:4-5). That was the proverbial line, if you have not guessed by now. Do I need to show you the sinker? Oh, why not. "And all the days that Adam lived were nine hundred and thirty years: and he died." (Genesis 5:5).

I would like to stop and point out here that this is not necessarily a true example of collateral damage. Death was the known price demanded as payment for Adam's disobedience to God. "Therefore we ought to give the more earnest heed to the things which we have heard, lest at any time we should let them slip. 2 For if the word spoken by angels was stedfast, and every transgression and disobedience received a just recompense of reward;" (Hebrews 2:1-2). The hook, line, and sinker of Satan's ulterior motive is your eventual death and separation from God. As for the remaining punishments God implemented after Adam and Eve dared to eat of the tree. This too, will cause unforeseen complications for them or collateral damage. Also, Adam and Eve should now discern a change in Creation since their eyes are open. There is circumstantial evidence that indicates their sinful actions will cause future generations to suffer. "Unto the woman he said, I will greatly multiply thy sorrow and thy conception; in sorrow thou shalt bring forth children; and thy desire shall be to thy husband, and he shall rule over thee. 17 And unto Adam he said, Because thou hast hearkened unto the voice of thy wife, and hast eaten of the tree, of which I commanded thee, saying, Thou shalt not eat of it: cursed is the ground for thy sake; in sorrow shalt thou eat of it all the days of thy life; 18 Thorns also and thistles shall it bring forth to thee; and thou shalt eat the herb of the field; 19 In the sweat of thy face shalt thou eat bread, till thou return unto the ground; for out of it wast thou taken: for dust thou art, and unto dust shalt thou return." (Genesis 3:16-19). I cannot begin to imagine how frightening God's words must have been to Adam at that moment, knowing he and Eve would die at some appointed time in the future. This was an unknown concept to Adam. He had never seen or experienced death. Remember, the threat of death was only associated with the tree of Knowledge. "But of the tree of the knowledge of good and evil, thou shalt not eat of it: for in the day that thou eatest thereof thou shalt surely die." (Genesis 2:17). And I think it is obvious that the threat of death was not a major deterrent for Adam, as it is now for us. We truly know the meaning of death. However, it stands to reason that Adam was left to wonder, "what was death?". Would it be painful? What was going to happen to them after they died? They had no clue, but that was about to change. I want to pause here and ask you to highlight Genesis chapter 3, verse 16, for I will address Eve's punishment in greater detail in the coming chapter Kingdom of Heaven.

Let's return to my earlier point. You might have questions regarding the circumstantial evidence that I said was present now that Adam and Eve's eyes have been opened. How could they possibly be aware of the collateral damage their sins would cause later generations? The hidden clues are there if you look for them; consider what God said in verse 16 of Genesis chapter 3. God told Eve she would bear children in sorrow. Therefore, she has to know that those children of the following generation will suffer because of her sins. But suffer what? The answer to that question is found in what God told Adam in verse 17 of Genesis chapter 3. God cursed the ground because of Adam's sins, and that curse, by default, would affect their children and future generations. And if you are wondering how a curse upon the ground could affect Adam's children? The explanation is simple and relatable, Food. Those children and future generations will have to contend with the thorns and thistles of the cursed ground, day after day, for it to produce a harvest.

The verse I will quote next may possibly contain the very act which revealed to Satan the significance of collateral damage. The innocent is about to suffer for the sins of the guilty. "Unto Adam also and to his wife did the Lord God make coats of skins, and clothed them." (Genesis 3:21). On the surface, most would conclude this verse was of little importance. Not true! God gave us a lot to unpack here, for what comes out of Adam's Pandora's box of sin is earth-shaking. First of all, we see God establish the practice of Animal Sacrifice, or the shedding of innocent blood to literally cover Man. This is a clear illustration of Jesus and God's Plan of Salvation. I said in chapter 2 that God could not show Adam and Eve mercy for their actions. But, what we do see here is the application of Grace by God toward Adam and Eve through this act of animal sacrifice. The Bible does not elaborate on which animal or animals were killed to provide clothing for Adam and Eve. It may have been a goat or a ram. However, what we do know, is, if Adam and Eve had obeyed God, there would not have been a need for the Animal's life to be forfeited. "And Aaron shall offer his bullock of the sin offering, which is for himself, and make an atonement for himself, and for his house. 34 And this shall be an everlasting statute unto you, to make an atonement for the children of Israel for all their sins once a year. And he did as the Lord commanded Moses." (Leviticus 16:6,34).

As every Believer knows, this is a temporary fix to a systemic problem that needs the permanent solution of Jesus. "But in those sacrifices there is a remembrance again made of sins every year. 4 For it is not possible that the blood of bulls and of goats should take away sins. 5 Wherefore when he cometh into the world, he saith, Sacrifice and offering thou wouldest not, but a body hast thou prepared me: 6 In burnt offerings and sacrifices for sin thou hast had no pleasure. 7 Then said I, Lo, I come (in the volume of the book it is written of me,) to do thy will, O God. 10 By the which will we are sanctified through the offering of the body of Jesus Christ once for all. 12 But this man, after he had offered one sacrifice for sins for ever, sat down on the right hand of God;" (Hebrews 10:3-7,10,12). I warned you. This was a lot to unpack. I do not wish to get too deep here. Still, when I view these scriptures through the Spirit, it becomes evident that these events were set into motion long before God said, "Let us make man." Also, if you have not developed the skill of reading in the Spirit, do not worry I will go into great detail about it in the coming chapters.

Satan now takes full advantage of this new weapon in his arsenal, collateral damage. And because of this, we, the Children of God, must never forget that our adversary Satan hates a family that walks in the ways of the Lord. "And if it seem evil unto you to serve the Lord, choose you this day whom ye will serve; whether the gods which your fathers served that were on the other side of the flood, or the gods of the Amorites, in whose land ye dwell: but as for me and my house, we will serve the Lord." (Joshua 24:15). Examine Satan's first attack on Man. He never attacked Adam while he was the sole human on the planet, nor did he attack Eve while she was alone. "And when the woman saw that the tree was good for food, and that it was pleasant to the eyes, and a tree to be desired to make one wise, she took of the fruit thereof, and did eat, and gave also unto her husband with her; and he did eat." (Genesis 3:6).

God shows us that Satan's first attack was perpetrated upon husband and wife – humanity's first family. Unfortunately, Adam and Eve will soon discover this will not be the last attack of Satan. "And Adam knew Eve his wife; and she conceived, and bare Cain, and said, I have gotten a man from the Lord. 2, And she again bare his brother Abel. And Abel was a keeper of sheep, but Cain was a tiller of the ground." (Genesis 4:1-2). Genesis chapter 4, reveals that Adam and Eve are making the best out of a bad situation. They are no longer living in paradise, but life must go on. Their little family was starting to grow, but with that growth came Satan. "And in process of time it came to pass, that Cain brought of the fruit of the ground an offering unto the Lord. 4 And Abel, he also brought of the firstlings of his flock and of the fat thereof. And the Lord had respect unto Abel and to his offering: 5 But unto Cain and to his offering he had not respect. And Cain was very wroth, and his countenance fell. 6 And the Lord said unto Cain, Why art thou wroth? and why is thy countenance fallen? 7 If thou doest well, shalt thou not be accepted? and if thou doest not well, sin lieth at the door. And unto thee shall be his desire, and thou shalt rule over him. 8 And Cain talked with Abel his brother: and it came to pass, when they were in the field, that Cain rose up against Abel his brother, and slew him." (Genesis 4:3-8).

In times past, before various safety protocols were implemented in coal mines across the country, coal miners developed a disease called Black Lung. This was a deadly condition a coal miner would develop by inhaling coal dust particles from the mining process. The miner's lungs would eventually become so scared by dust particles that taking a breath was laborious. In the end, the coal miner's condition would deteriorate to the point where inevitably, the miner would suffocate to death. Here's my point, according to Genesis chapter 4, verse 2, Cain was a tiller of the ground. This would be the same ground God cursed due to the sins of Cain's father, Adam. This leads me to believe there exists more than a plausible connection between that cursed ground and the act of the first murder committed. Cain worked the toxic ground day in and day out, undoubtedly covered from head to toe in that accursed soil. There seems to be present a physical and spiritual possibility of Cain's profession causing his unfortunate sinful decision. What we do know for certain is that the collateral damage from Adam and Eve's sins manifested in the death of their second-born son Abel. And his killer is their firstborn son Cain.

Here is another personal example. Before I was involved in Christian ministry, I had the opportunity to add a very profitable Liquor store to my business portfolio. But, my mother and father objected. They pointed out that I was raised as a Christian in a Christian family. I eventually agreed with my parents. I fully understood that I could not in good conscience own a business that contributed to the destruction of so many communities and families. I would ask you to take a good look at your profession. Is your Job a blessing or a curse to society? In my example, the coal miner lost his life because of the work he chose, but his profession never placed his soul in jeopardy. And yes, I know you may make a good living in your line of work, whatever that work may be, but is collateral damage to your community a residual side effect of your profession? "For what shall it profit a man, if he shall gain the whole world, and lose his own soul?" (Mark 8:36). The old Saints used to say, "if you give the Devil an inch, he will take a mile." They knew most people did not start their lives seeking to end them in Hell. No, the journey to Hell is a long, drawn-out series of circumstances and events that will place you and possibly those around you there. This is what sin does; it gets into everything and everyone it contacts. If you invite Satan into your life, you won't be able to get him out of your life. If you walk with the Devil for a second, he will take you too far away from the truth. And if you entertain the Devil, eventually, you will become his entertainment.

Take David, for example, and to be clear, I am not saying David went to Hell for his sins. However, I am saying that a series of events and circumstances made David's life a living Hell. "Now therefore the sword shall never depart from thine house; because thou hast despised me, and hast taken the wife of Uriah the Hittite to be thy wife." (2 Samuel 12:10). First, we find King David out of place, he was not where he was supposed to be at that time, the King's place was on the battlefield with his men. "And it came to pass, after the year was expired, at the time when kings go forth to battle, that David sent Joab, and his servants with him, and all Israel; and they destroyed the children of Ammon, and besieged Rabbah. But David tarried still at Jerusalem. 2 And it came to pass in an eveningtide, that David arose from off his bed, and walked upon the roof of the king's house: and from the roof he saw a woman washing herself; and the woman was very beautiful to look upon." (2 Samuel 11:1-2). As it stands with David, he is not at the point of no return. The Holy Spirit will always provide a Child of God an opportunity to exit a sinful situation. How often have you heard a soft voice tell you to leave a place or situation? A voice that says, you should not be here or tell you not to do something because it is wrong. That is God talking to you, and in the future, please listen to this voice because your Soul may not be able to afford what comes next. As all Believers know, David's relationship with Bathsheba directly violated God's Law. Bathsheba was not betrothed to the King; she was married to Uriah the Hittite, a faithful soldier in King David's army. "Thou shalt not covet thy neighbour's house, thou shalt not covet thy neighbour's wife, nor his manservant, nor his maidservant, nor his ox, nor his ass, nor any thing that is thy neighbour's" (Exodus 20:17). By breaking this commandment David opens the door for the first demon.

Let's observe that first demon at work. "And David sent messengers, and took her; and she came in unto him, and he lay with her; for she was purified from her uncleanness: and she returned unto her house. 5 And the woman conceived, and sent and told David, and said, I am with child. 6 And David sent to Joab, saying, Send me Uriah the Hittite. And Joab sent Uriah to David." (2 Samuel 11:4-6). OK, here's a checklist of the demonic forces present with David so far. We have the demon of lust, which brought the demon of adultery, which brought the demon of deception. "And when David had called him, he did eat and drink before him; and he made him drunk: and at even he went out to lie on his bed with the servants of his lord, but went not down to his house. 14 And it came to pass in the morning, that David wrote a letter to Joab, and sent it by the hand of Uriah. 15 And he wrote in the letter, saying, Set ye Uriah in the forefront of the hottest battle, and retire ye from him, that he may be smitten, and die." (2 Samuel 11:13-15). Now, the rest of the demonic team have arrived to reside within David. There is now a lying demon, which brought with him the demons of betrayal, immorality, and the final and most deadly demon, the demon of murder. I would also like to state that it stands to reason that the demons of hate and anger were probably present as well. Because of David's sin the collateral damage done unto him, his family, and the Kingdom of Israel was extensive. But, unbeknownst to David, a hidden reason exists concerning Satan's attack upon his life, which I will explain later.

Satan is not all-knowing nor omnipotent, but he does know Jesus and God's purpose for Jesus. "When Jesus had thus said, he was troubled in spirit, and testified, and said, Verily, verily, I say unto you, that one of you shall betray me. 22 Then the disciples looked one on another, doubting of whom he spake. 25 He then lying on Jesus' breast saith unto him, Lord, who is it? 26 Jesus answered, He it is, to whom I shall give a sop, when I have dipped it. And when he had dipped the sop, he gave it to Judas Iscariot, the son of Simon. 27 And after the sop Satan entered into him. Then said Jesus unto him, That thou doest, do quickly." (John 13:21-22,25-27). However, Satan did not know or consider that the collateral damage from Judas' action would work against him. "And I, if I be lifted up from the earth, will draw all men unto me." (John 12:32). Satan now sees the power of the Cross. Because of this knowledge, Satan hates us and our offspring, or as the Bible calls us, the Sons of Man. Satan is fully aware that children represent the next generation of Believers. He also knows that there will eventually arise a generation that will usher in the return of Christ. This is why Satan attempts to brutalize and destroy as many fathers as possible. He wants them absent or completely out of the lives of their children.

Once, early on in our marriage, my wife and I had a bad argument. I don't remember what the argument was about but I do remember it upset our toddler terribly. It was at that point, my wife and I realized what Satan was up to. The Devil knows he cannot rob me or my wife of our salvation, but if he can deny it for our children, this would be a victory nonetheless. My wife and I are saved and sold out to the Lord. We are determined to endure until the end. "For I am persuade, that neither death, nor life, nor angels, nor principalities, nor powers, nor things present, nor things to come, 39 Nor height, nor depth, nor any other creature, shall be able to separate us from the love of God, which is in Christ Jesus our Lord." (Romans 8:38-39). However, we do know that if something happened to our marriage, it could make our children vulnerable to Satan's attacks, placing their salvation in jeopardy. I know marriage can be difficult. Each will have its own countless trials and tribulations. In addition, some of us have chosen to marry people from different backgrounds and cultures. Arguments and disagreements will inevitably occur. But, if we never forget God's love for us both, the love for our spouse is more likely to endure. We must do whatever it takes to resolve all arguments, disagreements, and misunderstandings before they fester into something that sickens our marriage. And we know all too well that these disagreements can become Irreconcilable. "Be ye angry, and sin not: let not the sun go down upon your wrath:" (Ephesians 4:26). Dear readers, seriously ask yourself, is there anything Satan can do or offer you worth the Collateral Damage that will eventually fall upon you and your children? I think you know the answer to this question.

"Every good gift and every perfect gift is from above, and cometh down from the Father of lights, with whom is no variableness, neither shadow of turning." (James 1:17).

Chapter Four

THE DEVIL YOU KNOW

"For from within, out of the heart of men, proceed evil thoughts, adulteries, fornications, murders, 22 Thefts, covetousness, wickedness, deceit, lasciviousness, an evil eye, blasphemy, pride, foolishness: 23 All these evil things come from within, and defile the man." (Mark 7:21-23).

I have come to an unfortunate and unsettling realization - the most dangerous person on the planet is, in many cases, the person closest to you. That special someone that is with you every second of every day of your life. The person who knows all your secrets and where every skeleton is buried. This person knows your strengths and weaknesses. He knows what you like and what you don't like. This person knows your fears, what keeps you up at night; he knows your innermost thoughts. And if that was not frightening enough, his actions could lead you straight to Hell. Who could this be? Who is this backstabbing frenemy? Please do not panic, but he is with you right now. Uncovering this terrible individual takes one action - a long look in the mirror. I know it is troubling, and I truly hate to be the bearer of bad news, my friends. But you are frankly your own worst enemy. "For the flesh lusteth against the Spirit, and the Spirit against the flesh: and these are contrary the one to the other: so that ye cannot do the things that ye would. 19 Now the works of the flesh are manifest, which are these; Adultery, fornication, uncleanness, lasciviousness, 20 Idolatry, witchcraft, hatred, variance, emulations, wrath, strife, seditions, heresies, 21 Envyings, murders, drunkenness, revellings, and such like: of the which I tell you before, as I have also told you in time past, that they which do such things shall not inherit the kingdom of God." (Galatians 5:17,19-21).

In theater, sociology, and psychology, the hurdles above are described as a "narrative conflict" between you and yourself. In the spirit world, being controlled by the hurdles mentioned above means your narrative (your life) belongs to Satan. Take a minute or two to process all of this, but once you come to this understanding, you will be better. You are being targeted as a Manchurian Candidate by Satan to play Russian Roulette with your Soul. Imagine what a wonderful world this would have been if Adam and Eve had only walked away from the lying serpent. Paradise would have been ours if they had only said to the serpent, no thanks we are not hungry. What if they had done what I have advised others to do many times - check with God first? "But seek ye first the kingdom of God, and his righteousness; and all these things shall be added unto you." (Matthew 6:33). I won't continue to bash our forefathers, Adam and Eve, because we are not much better ourselves. In most cases, not all but most, we have done such horrible things and herald them as good. All manners of ungodly behavior, so much so that we or others have been scarred for life. Every heart you have broken: every wicked decision you have ever made, every wrong road you have ever traveled, and every unkind act you have created. You have done these things of your own accord. Every heinous crime you have committed: every lie you have ever told, every betrayal you have chosen not to forgive, you made the conscious decision to do so at Satan's behest. In the scriptures, the Apostle Paul uses himself as an example. "O wretched man that I am! who shall deliver me from the body of this death?" (Romans 7:24).

Paul pronounces the difficulties of this Christian walk to the Believer. The flesh was the main character or leading lady in those past behaviors and practices. Many of which were strongholds for spiritual disasters in our previous life. Yes, our previous life is the proverbial skeleton in the closet, the constant annoying thorn in our side. Christians must always remember their flaws and confess those faults one to another. We must not give Satan leeway to use our past as a weapon, by trying to hide who we once were. He knows you cheated on your husband because he was the Devil you cheated with. Satan knows you once had a problem with drugs because he was your drug dealer. This is a tried and true tactic of the Devil; he wants to vilify you by using who you once were as an example against who you are now. The Apostle Paul demonstrates confession is the best tool we can use to defeat this type of self-deprecating evil. "For I am the least of the apostles, that am not meet to be called an apostle, because I persecuted the church of God." (1 Corinthians 15:9). Your past is just that, your past; he is no more because you have been Born Again. "Therefore if any man be in Christ, he is a new creature: old things are passed away; behold, all things are become new." (2 Corinthians 5:17). Please highlight this amazing scripture. We will take a closer look at this new creature later.

All Pastors know the most fragile period in a Believer's spiritual life is when they are first converted. "When the unclean spirit is gone out of a man, he walketh through dry places, seeking rest, and findeth none. 44 Then he saith, I will return into my house from whence I came out; and when he is come, he findeth it empty, swept, and garnished. 45 Then goeth he, and taketh with himself seven other spirits more wicked than himself, and they enter in and dwell there: and the last state of that man is worse than the first. Even so shall it be also unto this wicked generation." (Matthew 12:43-45). It is well known among the righteous that Satan becomes exceedingly active in the life of a new convert. Because, the Devil knows he is about to lose another Soul to God.

Yes, our Soul, the ultimate prize, the rarest, most valuable jewel in the crown of creation. No man has ever seen his Soul, no one has ever held it, you cannot buy it, and you cannot sell it, but you can give it away. The Soul is the final piece of the puzzle. What is a Man's Soul? This question is not easily answered. It has perplexed Man since the beginning of time. The Bible does not provide a definitive answer to what the Soul is, so we must extrapolate. First, your Soul is eternal. It is who you are at your core. Second, the recipe of your Soul is your essence, your psyche or mind. Throw in your emotions and willpower; there you have it, your Soul. Third, value is placed upon it by God and Satan. It would be best if you strived to take better care of your own valuable Soul. And I know of no better caretaker than Jesus Christ.

This creates an interesting point. Since Man was made in the image and likeness of God, Man can also be described as a Trinity. We are a living Spirit, we have a living Soul, and those two separate entities are placed inside an earthly vessel called the Body. As you can see, a true Trinity. For he is Body, Spirit, and Soul. This brings me to another point: your body and mind are the battlefields for a bloodless but agonizing fight between God and Satan. The Apostle Paul characterizes this fight in the scriptures. "For the good that I would I do not: but the evil which I would not, that I do. 20 Now if I do that I would not, it is no more I that do it, but sin that dwelleth in me. 21 I find then a law, that, when I would do good, evil is present with me. 22 For I delight in the law of God after the inward man: 23 But I see another law in my members, warring against the law of my mind, and bringing me into captivity to the law of sin which is in my members." (Romans 7:19-23). This scripture should be required reading for all Believers. The reason is when you are at war, you must be able to identify the enemy, even if that enemy is you.

As a Christian, your first fight with the Devil will likely be an internal fight with yourself. And trust me, if you are going to be truly successful as a Christian, this is a fight you must win time and time again. You will not have total success in denying the Devil if you cannot first deny yourself. "From that time forth began Jesus to shew unto his disciples, how that he must go unto Jerusalem, and suffer many things of the elders and chief priests and scribes, and be killed, and be raised again the third day. 22 Then Peter took him, and began to rebuke him, saying, Be it far from thee, Lord: this shall not be unto thee. 23 But he turned, and said unto Peter, Get thee behind me, Satan: thou art an offense unto me: for thou savourest not the things that be of God, but those that be of men. 24 Then said Jesus unto his disciples, If any man will come after me, let him deny himself, and take up his cross, and follow me." (Matthew 16:21-24). Often, we only look at those things we consider bad behavior as the things we should deny (e.g., drugs, alcohol, premarital sex). However, according to verse 22 of Matthew chapter 16, Jesus admonished Peter for behavior many would consider admirable. After all, who doesn't want a friend who would fight to keep him from harm? Much of our behavior in this world is based on qualities humanity finds desirable, but spiritually they are in direct opposition with what God considers appropriate. "Woe unto you, when all men shall speak well of you! for so did their fathers to the false prophets." (Luke 6:26). As you can see, we are to deny ourselves not only of bad behavior but also of narratives we pride ourselves in as well.

Wars are often composed of many different types of battles. Some battles were considered as small skirmishes, while others were huge engagements. History has shown us that some battles have been fought that at the time of the engagement, appeared to have had little or no strategic importance whatsoever. However, historians later discovered the entire war hinged on the outcome of that small insignificant battle. “And the Lord said unto Gideon, By the three hundred men that lapped will I save you, and deliver the Midianites into thine hand: and let all the other people go every man unto his place.” (Judges 7:7).

Let's look at the Apostle Paul again; it is evident that Paul was not your typical Christian. Case in point, Jesus did make a special trip back to Earth to convert the guy. "And Saul, yet breathing out threatenings and slaughter against the disciples of the Lord, went unto the high priest, 2 And desired of him letters to Damascus to the synagogues, that if he found any of this way, whether they were men or women, he might bring them bound unto Jerusalem. 3 And as he journeyed, he came near Damascus: and suddenly there shined round about him a light from heaven: 4 And he fell to the earth, and heard a voice saying unto him, Saul, Saul, why persecutest thou me? 5 And he said, Who art thou, Lord? And the Lord said, I am Jesus whom thou persecutest: it is hard for thee to kick against the pricks. 6 And he trembling and astonished said, Lord, what wilt thou have me to do? And the Lord said unto him, Arise, and go into the city, and it shall be told thee what thou must do." (Acts 9:1-6). To Paul's credit, he is known to have written half of the New Testament Bible. However, in the kingdom of God, Paul is no greater than you. He must also look in the mirror. "For there is no respect of persons with God." (Romans 2:11). God has made available to us the same tools, if not more than Paul had available to him at the time of his service. Although it appears, we keep misplacing the toolbox. This brings me to my next point, why do believers work against what is obviously in our best interest - the spreading of the Gospel Message? We continue to dilute the Word of God through our ungodly actions and bad behavior. We are constantly shooting ourselves in the foot. Earlier in this chapter, I reference the converted Paul as my example, not the pre-Damascus Road unconverted Saul. My basis here is that Paul was a Christian, just as we are Christians. What I truly find troubling in this day and age is not the behavior of the sinner but the behavior of the Saint. The behavior of the Saint has become the behavior of the sinner. The sinner, or the Children of darkness, are doing what they have been assigned. The killer is killing: the liar is lying, the cheat is cheating, the thief is stealing, and the Devil is most definitely getting the glory. Remember, in the Introduction section of this Book, I quoted Isaiah chapter 5 verse 14, which stated, "Hell has enlarged herself." The reason for the expansion project is Hell was never created for the Sons of Men. It was initially created for the Sons of God, or as we know them, the fallen angels who betrayed God and followed Satan. "For if God spared not the angels that sinned, but cast them down to hell, and delivered them into chains of darkness, to be reserved unto judgment" (2 Peter 2:4). When you seriously view the world in which we live today, it becomes quite evident, that the Children of Satan are literally working overtime to fill every nook and cranny in Hell. So, it stands to reason that the Children of God should be working just as diligently to fill every Mansion in Heaven!

What demonic factors are to blame for the lack of commitment from the followers of Christ Jesus? As I stated in the previous chapter, Satan plays an acutely long game. He has implemented a distraction strategy that causes Christians to obsess with the concerns and cares of this world. This particular strategy of Satan has been so successful against Christians that it has caused us to lose sight of our main objective. What is our main objective? Simple; Child of God you were saved to save someone. "Go ye therefore, and teach all nations, baptizing them in the name of the Father, and of the Son, and of the Holy Ghost:" (Matthew 28:19) The Great Commission is imperative to God's Plan of Salvation. As Believers, we cannot afford to lose focus of this glorious assignment. Especially not over the temporary adornments of this world. And, it is all temporary. Please refer back to Revelation's chapter 21, verse 1. It states that there will be a new Earth in our future, and the old Earth will pass away. Anything contained in or on the old Earth will be eliminated. This means all wealth and all status will cease to exist. The gold in the hills: the diamonds in the ground, the cash in your 401k, and the stocks in your portfolio will have no real value. Every country: every kingdom, every political office, every political power, and every feeble title

Man has ever held will be abolished. Only the things we have done for God will last when the end comes, and it will come. "But what things were gain to me, those I counted loss for Christ. 8 Yea doubtless, and I count all things but loss for the excellency of the knowledge of Christ Jesus my Lord: for whom I have suffered the loss of all things, and do count them but dung, that I may win Christ," (Philippians 3:7-8).

Satan is not deploying a new tactic here. On the contrary, he is using the same old bag of tricks against us that he has used in the past. Satan sends the proverbial other woman when he wants to destroy a man and his marriage. When the Devil wants to destroy a woman, he toys with her emotions. Will someone please explain to me how the Devil is still winning the war with these old weapons? He seems to beat us at every turn. Jesus did not succumb to Satan's temptations, so why are we? "And Jesus being full of the Holy Ghost returned from Jordan, and was led by the Spirit into the wilderness, 2 Being forty days tempted of the devil. And in those days he did eat nothing: and when they were ended, he afterward hungered. 3 And the devil said unto him, if thou be the Son of God, command this stone that it be made bread. 4 And Jesus answered him, saying, it is written, That Man shall not live by bread alone, but by every word of God. 5 And the devil, taking him up into an high mountain, shewed unto him all the kingdoms of the world in a moment of time. 6 And the devil said unto him, All this power will I give thee, and the glory of them: for that is delivered unto me; and to whomsoever I will I give it. 7 If thou therefore wilt worship me, all shall be thine. 8 And Jesus answered and said unto him, Get thee behind me, Satan: for it is written, Thou shalt worship the Lord thy God, and him only shalt thou serve. 9 And he brought him to Jerusalem, and set him on a pinnacle of the temple, and said unto him, if thou be the Son of God, cast thyself down from hence: 10 For it is written, He shall give his angels charge over thee, to keep thee: 11 And in their hands they shall bear thee up, lest at any time thou dash thy foot against a stone. 12 And Jesus answering

said unto him, It is said, Thou shalt not tempt the Lord thy God.
13 And when the devil had ended all the temptation, he departed
from him for a season." (Luke 4:1-13).

Since the temptation of Christ by Satan is so vitally important to us, the followers of Jesus, I chose to quote the text in its entirety. Verse 1 has answered my question: How is Satan defeating us at every turn? As followers of Christ, we must be led by the same power that led Jesus, the Holy Ghost. Without the Holy Spirit, we have no power. And if a Christian has no power, he will have no true Victory. I will discuss the Holy Ghost in greater detail in the chapter called The Spirit of the Matter. Luke further guides the Believer through an in-depth review of Satan's main tactics and how it is deployed against the Children of God. Luke also provides insight into what happens to a person if he follows Satan's instructions. "Know ye not, that to whom ye yield yourselves servants to obey, his servants ye are to whom ye obey; whether of sin unto death, or of obedience unto righteousness?" (Romans 6:16). Case in point, verse 9 if read in the spirit reveals to the reader, that death is Satan's ultimate goal for those who would choose to listen or serve him. Satan told Jesus to cast himself down from the top of the Temple. Had Jesus done as Satan had instructed and jumped, this would have been an act of spiritual suicide, if not physical suicide as well. Because we do not necessarily know if Satan would have kept his word and lifted Jesus after he had jumped. After all, he is known as the father of lies.

The Bible supports my position on Satan's suicide tactics; other scriptures also verify this theory. "Then Judas, which had betrayed him, when he saw that he was condemned, repented himself, and brought again the thirty pieces of silver to the chief priest and elders, 4 Saying, I have sinned in that I have betrayed the innocent blood. And they said, What is that to us? see thou to that. 5 And he cast down the piece of silver in the temple, and departed, and went and hanged himself." (Matthew 27:3-5). In addition, the Bible also describes what appears to be a suicide attempt by the prophet Jonah. "Now the word of the Lord came unto Jonah the son of Amittai, saying, 2 Arise, go to Nineveh, that great city, and cry against it; for their wickedness is come up before me. 3 But Jonah rose up to flee unto Tarshish from the presence of the Lord, and went down to Joppa; and he found a ship going to Tarshish: so he paid the fare thereof, and went down into it, to go with them unto Tarshish from the presence of the Lord. 4 But the Lord sent out a great wind into the sea, and there was a mighty tempest in the sea, so that the ship was like to be broken. 7 And they said every one to his fellow, Come, and let us cast lots, that we may know for whose cause this evil is upon us. So they cast lots, and the lot fell upon Jonah. 11 Then said they unto him, What shall we do unto thee, that the sea may be calm unto us? for the sea wrought, and was tempestuous. 12 And he said unto them, Take me up, and cast me forth into the sea; so shall the sea be calm unto you: for I know that for my sake this great tempest is upon you. 15 So they took up Jonah, and cast him forth into the sea: and the sea ceased from her raging." (Jonah 1:1-4,7,11-12,15). These scriptures also suggest that suicide is not always a sign of mental illness. In some rare cases, it can be a sign of a greater spiritual battle.

In this world, we have seen other ways Satan gets us to harm ourselves. I will use the conditional circumstances God put into place at Creation as my example. "And God said, Let the earth bring forth grass, the herb yielding seed, and the fruit tree yielding fruit after his kind, whose seed is in itself, upon the earth: and it was so. 20 And God said, Let the waters bring forth abundantly the moving creature that hath life, and fowl that may fly above the earth in the open firmament of heaven. 21 And God created great whales, and every living creature that moveth, which the waters brought forth abundantly, after their kind, and every winged fowl after his kind: and God saw that it was good." (Genesis 1:11,20-21). Have you ever considered, as long as what God created stayed connected to what it was created from or for; continues to have life?

However, if that connection is severed, it dies. If you take the fish from the water, it dies. If you pull the grass from the ground, it dies. If you take the eagle from the sky and place it under the sea, it dies. Likewise, if you separate Man from the God that created him and used His breath to give him life, he too shalt surely die. Always remember, sin separates us from God the Creator. "And the Lord God formed man of the dust of the ground, and breath into his nostrils the breath of life; and man became a living soul. 17 But of the tree of the knowledge of good and evil, thou shalt not eat of it: for in the day that thou eatest thereof thou shalt surely die." (Genesis 2:7,17).

I have had the misfortune to know individuals who have slowly killed themselves with drugs and alcohol. Never could they have imagined their first use of these substances would one day eventually end at their grave. I am not taking substance abuse or suicide lightly. I fully understand the devastating effects that substance abuse and suicide have had on many families within our communities and society. If you or someone you know feels that suicide is a viable option, please call the National Suicide Prevention Lifeline at 800-273-8255. Help is available. I believe these scriptures and the examples I have provided will strengthen us, and provide a better understanding of the many ways Satan tries to defeat us. Jesus and Paul defeated the Devil, no matter which tactics Satan chose to deploy. These verses will also equip us with the necessary skills and abilities to defeat him. "Then the devil leaveth him, and, behold, angels came and ministered unto him." (Matthew 4:11). In treating addictions, many Psychologists believe the first step to recovery begins when you recognize you have a problem. Likewise, we must also realize that we too have a problem. We are all sinners, it is who we are. It is embedded in our DNA, and it is because of this fact that we do not have the power to save ourselves.

The major difference between Christianity and other Religions is Christianity takes the burden of salvation out of our hands and places it squarely upon Jesus Christ. "Neither is there salvation in any other: for there is none other name under heaven given among men, whereby we must be saved." (Acts 4:12). If you are reading this book, you have probably made this first step and accepted Christ Jesus as your Lord in Savior, but as the old Saints use to say, "If there be any sinners in the house - you need Jesus." Having said that, salvation is here. Read this verse and follow my instructions. "That if thou shalt confess with thy mouth the Lord Jesus, and shalt believe in thine heart that God hath raised him from the dead, thou shalt be saved." (Romans 10:9). Now please repeat this. I believe that Jesus Christ the only begotten Son of God died on the Cross for my sins. And on the third day, God raised him from the grave for the remission of my sins. Jesus, I accept you as my Lord and Savior. Amen. If you repeated that last statement and truly believed it, congratulation. You, my friend, are now saved. Although you may not yet realize it, you have just scored a major victory against the devil you know. Let me be the first one to welcome you into the Faith. Please find a Bible-based Church to attend and perform your Baptism. You have now started traveling the path of righteousness that leads to Heaven. And please never forget, you are not alone. We are all praying for you. "Because strait is the gate, and narrow is the way, which leadeth unto life, and few there be that find it." (Matthew 7:14).

Every person on the planet has experienced an event or events in their life that may have left them scarred. In some people, they are emotional or mental, and in others, they are physical. In some severe cases, it runs the gamut. For many of us, those scars have been the source of great pain, sorrow, and anger. This yoke has tormented us, knocked us down, and driven some to alcohol or drug use. And, in extreme cases, those scars have caused some of us to scar others. Damaged people will inevitably damage people. This is the World in which we live, it seems void of any reason. It will hurt you, and it's not fair. It stopped being fair after Adam sinned. Remember the innocent animal that had to forfeit its life to provide clothing for Adam and Eve. I cannot begin to imagine the ordeals that some of you have endured. However, it would be best to not let your scars define you. Yes, they are your truth. Nevertheless, you must not allow that truth to keep you from moving forward into a resting place in the Lord. "Come unto me, all ye that labour and are heavy laden, and I will give you rest." (Matthew 11:28).

Satan has purposely placed cruel and mean-spirited people in your life. They are the ones that have hurt you and caused you so much pain, their primary goal is to stop you from reaching the destination God has chosen for you. Jesus taught his disciples about this type of behavior. He described it in his parable about a sower sowing seeds. "A sower went out to sow his seed: and as he sowed, some fell by the way side; and it was trodden down, and the fowls of the air devoured it. 6 And some fell upon a rock; and as soon as it was sprung up, it withered away, because it lacked moisture. 7 And some fell among thorns; and the thorns sprang up with it, and choked it. 8 And other fell on good ground, and sprang up, and bare fruit an hundredfold. And when he had said these things, he cried, He that hath ears to hear, let him hear. 9 And his disciples asked him, saying, What might this parable be? 10 And he said, Unto you it is given to know the mysteries of the kingdom of God: but to others in parables; that seeing they might not see, and hearing they might not understand. 11 Now the parable is this: The seed is the word of God. 12 Those by the way side are they that hear; then cometh the devil, and taketh away the word out of their hearts, lest they should believe and be saved." (Luke 8:5-12).

The pain and damage from your past can take such a toll. You cannot allow the scars of the past to disfigure you. If left unresolved, it could very well jeopardize the future God has created for you. When you believe pain and suffering are all you have ever known and take refuge in that knowledge, all is lost.

The following is a biblical example of that type of damage and the negative effects it can have on people. The Children of Israel have now arrived at the land that God had promised them. But, because all they knew was hardship, they believed and behaved as if hardship was around every corner. They refused to crossover into a land flowing with milk and honey. Opting instead to launch a campaign to return to Egypt - the land of their bondage. Due to their emotional and mental scars, God did not allow them to enter into the Promise Land. "And all the children of Israel murmured against Moses and against Aaron: and the whole congregation said unto them, Would God that we had died in the land of Egypt! or would God we had died in this wilderness! 3 And wherefore hath the Lord brought us unto this land, to fall by the sword, that our wives and our children should be a prey? were it not better for us to return into Egypt? 4 And they said one to another, Let us make a captain, and let us return into Egypt." (Numbers 14:2-4). It is hard to believe that those who had been in bondage for hundreds of years. Made it to within yards of a new and blessed beginning, only to fail at the finish line. The Children of Israel were not defeated by Pharaoh or some powerful military force. No, they allowed the enemies in their own minds to rob them of a sure and guaranteed victory. And those emotional demons kept them from receiving a glorious inheritance from the Lord God.

Also, your own traditions can act as a stumbling block, hindering your efforts to finish God's race. Traditions are fickle; here is another interesting narrative to exemplify my point. Sadly, your grandfather was an alcoholic, and the men in your family believed it was a rite of passage to celebrate a son's eighteenth birthday by buying them their very first drink. Your grandfather sadly continued this tradition with your father, who unfortunately enjoyed it. Over time your father became an abusive alcoholic, and now he wants to celebrate your eighteenth birthday with the traditional first drink. Your father and grandfather were indeed both alcoholics, but this tradition does not have to become your truth. You could help mend the scars created by traditions by not scarring anyone else. If you do drink, do not drink in front of your children. If you smoke cigarettes or weed, please do not smoke in the presence of your children. And if you are prone to profanity, please refrain from cursing around your little children because it is exactly that, a curse.

I have some trepidation about this next example because it is controversial. There is a vile presence lurking in the Faith, and it most definitely does not belong within the Congregation of God's Children. There is only one reason it is present among Christians today. Once again, it is those wicked ways spoken about in 2nd Chronicles chapter 7, verse 14. I must address this specific Sin. For I proclaim I am one of God's Preachers, and I stand and preach His word to whom He would have me preach. “Preach the word; be instant in season, out of season; reprove, rebuke, exhort with all long suffering and doctrine.” (2 Timothy 4:2). Through the lasting effects of this tradition, Satan has gotten so many victories out of this particular sin. If it goes unchecked, it could cause irrevocable damage to the Faith. "And Jesus knew their thoughts, and said unto them, Every kingdom divided against itself is brought to desolation; and every city or house divided against itself shall not stand:" (Matthew 12:25). The tradition I am speaking of is Racism. Racism is so prevalent in America that our Nation's enemies are using it to destroy us without launching a single missile or firing a shot. Look at what took place in the year 2020. Our enemies are destroying us from within. And, I repeat, not only is this tradition of Racism jeopardizing our Country, it is jeopardizing the Church. "Making the word of God of none effect through your tradition, which ye have delivered: and many such like things do ye." (Mark 7:13).

Satan used carnal-minded theologians, merchants, and politicians in the 17th and 18th centuries to push forward the Curse Theory. This evil demonic theory helped perpetuate Slavery in America. Reverend Martin Luther King Jr. preached that the Curse of Ham theory was blasphemous and an insult to the Faith.

"And Noah began to be an husbandman, and he planted a vineyard: 21 And he drank of the wine, and was drunken; and he was uncovered within his tent. 22 And Ham, the father of Canaan, saw the nakedness of his father, and told his two brethren without. 23 And Shem and Japheth took a garment, and laid it upon both their shoulders, and went backward, and covered the nakedness of their father; and their faces were backward, and they saw not their father's nakedness. 24 And Noah awoke from his wine, and knew what his younger son had done unto him. 25 And he said, Cursed be Canaan; a servant of servants shall he be unto his brethren. 26 And he said, Blessed be the Lord God of Shem; and Canaan shall be his servant. 27 God shall enlarge Japheth, and he shall dwell in the tents of Shem; and Canaan shall be his servant." (Genesis 9:20-27).

Not only did Jesus teach on the subject of Racism, he also led by example with the woman at the well scripture. "Now Jacob's well was there. Jesus therefore, being wearied with his journey, sat thus on the well: and it was about the sixth hour. 7 There cometh a woman of Samaria to draw water: Jesus saith unto her, Give me to drink. 8 (For his disciples were gone away unto the city to buy meat.) 9 Then saith the woman of Samaria unto him, How is it that thou, being a Jew, askest drink of me, which am a woman of Samaria? for the Jews have no dealings with the Samaritans. 10 Jesus answered and said unto her, If thou knewest the gift of God, and who it is that saith to thee, Give me to drink; thou wouldest have asked of him, and he would have given thee living water." (John 4:6-10). Also, Paul addressed this subject matter in the New Testament Epistles. He provided clear insight into what our Father thinks about Race, Class, and Gender. "There is neither Jew nor Greek, there is neither bond nor free, there is neither male nor female: for ye are all one in Christ Jesus." (Galatians 3:28).

To be one in Christ Jesus means; we have more in common than even the Angels in Heaven, for we have been washed in the blood of the Lamb. If the blood Jesus shed on Calvary does not bond us as brothers and sisters, then nothing ever will.

Do you have traditions, beliefs, customs, habits, biases, or scars that keep you from offering the Living Water of Christ to someone? Maybe it was because someone did not look like you, or they did not behave and carry themselves like anyone you knew or would like to know. Have you not carried the Living Water of Christ to someone you felt lived in the wrong part of town? Were you not about your Father's business because you deemed the person to unworthy or they did not have a proper education nor did they possess a respectable pedigree? I am not here to argue whether "America is racist." What I am here to say, is, if the tradition of Racism has scarred your Christian brothers and sisters, that is sufficient enough for us, the Children of God, to take up their cause and strive to alleviate those grievances. "Now I beseech you, brethren, by the name of our Lord Jesus Christ, that ye all speak the same thing, and that there be no divisions among you; but that ye be perfectly joined together in the same mind and in the same judgment." (1 Corinthians 1:10). Examine yourself, is a small part of who you are the larger carnal parts of someone else? Do you often use terms like, "my mother said this or my father would say that"? Have others ever said you are the spitting image of your father or you have your mother's nature? I am not saying there is anything wrong with these types of comparisons. What I am saying, is you need to be certain of who or what is the source from which your mother and father draw upon. Is it Adam, or is it Jesus? "What mean ye, that ye use this proverb concerning the land of Israel, saying, The fathers have eaten sour grapes, and the children's teeth are set on edge?" (Ezekiel 18:2).

Here, Ezekiel quote's a proverb his people would often use to explain the origins of a sinful child. They believed the sins of the father could pass directly to the child. They were not too far off, well, maybe just a little short-sighted, because the Bible teaches us that all sin can be traced back to our father, Adam. Refer back to Chapter 2, The Fight Begins. The scripture I quoted about this matter is in Romans chapter 5, verse 12.

Jesus has shown his followers through his teachings that he understands the burden of family, especially if they are not anchored in the same spiritual foundation as you. "Then came to him his mother and his brethren, and could not come at him for the press. 20 And it was told him by certain which said, Thy mother and thy brethren stand without, desiring to see thee. 21 And he answered and said unto them, My mother and my brethren are these which hear the word of God, and do it." (Luke 8:19-21). Remember what was said in the last chapter Collateral Damage: the actions of others, including family, can cause great harm. I can give you chapters and verses on various topics dealing with pain, heartbreak, and betrayal in the Bible. The stories of Joseph, Ruth, and Samson, come to mind, but I am pretty sure you already know those scriptures. What I will say is Jesus can ease a troubled mind if you let him. "Casting all your care upon him; for he careth for you." (1 Peter 5:7). It is through Jesus and Jesus only that we can overcome our obstacles and the many pitfalls Satan has placed in our path. "Ye are of God, little children, and have overcome them: because greater is he that is in you, than he that is in the world." (1 John 4:4). I know it is hard for some of us to believe, that we have won the battle and the victory is ours. When many of us take account of our lives and view our surroundings, it is not a perfect picture of triumphs; nevertheless, claim yourself Victorious if you be in Christ. "But thanks be to God, which giveth us the victory through our Lord Jesus Christ." (1 Corinthians 15:57).

There is an old saying, "it's not what you know, it's who you know." We have seen countless examples of this in our society. We have all pondered at one time or another how a certain someone made it as far as they have with what little they know. Recently, I watched a famous person get interviewed on a late-night cable show. The show's host was heaping much praise upon his famous guest. But to my surprise, the famous person would not take credit for his success; he stated it had little to do with him and more with his family's last name. Have you ever truly considered the family into which you were reborn? "That which is born of the flesh is flesh; and that which is born of the Spirit is spirit." (John 3:6). You are a Child of God. You were born of the most powerful being in all of Creation - the Father. "Wherefore thou art no more a servant, but a son; and if a son, then an heir of God through Christ." (Galatians 4:7). I once heard a Sermon in which the Pastor stated, "our Father God is so rich, that He does not count His cattle, He counts the hills His cattle graze upon." "For every beast of the forest is mine, and the cattle upon a thousand hills." (Psalm 50:10).

It is imperative that we understand who Jesus is to the Father and what Jesus is to us. The Bible demonstrates that demons know and understand who Jesus is, so it is all the more reason for us to know him truly. "And there was in their synagogue a man with an unclean spirit; and he cried out, 24 Saying, Let us alone; what have we to do with thee, thou Jesus of Nazareth? art thou come to destroy us? I know thee who thou art, the Holy One of God." (Mark 1:23-24). Never forget that the Bible contains promises and blessings for those who love and obey the Word of God.

"Come now, and let us reason together, saith the Lord: though your sins be as scarlet, they shall be as white as snow; though they be red like crimson, they shall be as wool. 19 If ye be willing and obedient, ye shall eat the good of the land:" (Isaiah 1:18-19)

CHAPTER FIVE
THE DEVIL IN DISGUISE

"Then said Jesus unto the twelve, Will ye also go away? 68 Then Simon Peter answered him, Lord, to whom shall we go? thou hast the words of eternal life. 69 And we believe and are sure that thou art that Christ, the Son of the living God. 70 Jesus answered them, Have not I chosen you twelve, and one of you is a devil? 71 He spake of Judas Iscariot the son of Simon: for he it was that should betray him, being one of the twelve." (John 6:67-71).

We live in a day and age where trusting someone may cause you to lose your identity and your life savings. Trusting a lifelong friend could end a marriage because of an adulterous affair with a vulnerable spouse. And, in some extreme cases, trusting the wrong person in your inner circle may cost you your very life. What makes these cases all the more tragic is that the betrayal is not from your sworn enemy; it's not someone you crossed many years ago now seeking revenge. No, this Devil has disguised himself in the person of your wife: your husband, your brother, your best friend, or maybe your own parents or child.

When the police receive a missing person report concerning a wife, they will start their investigation for the missing woman with her husband. This has become what they call standard operating procedure. The police will inquire about the husband's whereabouts for the last twenty-four hours. They want to know about his state of mind, have there been any recent arguments or notable discord between the husband and the missing wife. The authorities will examine the husband's phone records and also his internet searches. They will ask his family, friends, and neighbors about his emotional state. The Detectives in charge of the search will seek to find out if the couple had a healthy relationship. Sadly, in many cases, the wife is found dead, and statistically, the evidence collected in the case usually points to the husband as the perpetrator of the crime. I cannot begin to imagine the horror the poor wife must have experienced during the last minutes of her life. The incomprehensible thoughts she must have had when she realized her husband and the father of her children was also the Demon that would end her life. Satan knows this blindsiding betrayal will destroy a family. Can you imagine the emotional and mental strain on the couple's children? The woman who gave them life, raised and cared for them, their mother, who they love, has been murdered. And the man who taught them how to ride a bike and drive a car, their father, who they once considered their hero, is now the Devil that has taken their mother's life. Family members try to recollect previous interactions with the couple. Did they miss any signs of abuse? Were there any noticeable changes in the husband's behavior? They want answers. They plead for someone to explain the motive, which might help them understand how their brother-in-law could be, the fun-loving uncle they visited for the Holidays. And, also the deceiver who committed this heinous crime. Sin is too small of a word to cover the gaping hole left in their lives.

Many would passively and respectfully say, "I guess it's just human nature," but the deceased's family wants a more plausible explanation that will provide some closure. But what explanation would be sufficient enough? What answer could be given that would appease a father's troubled mind? Knowing the man, he once treated as a son and gave his daughter's hand in marriage on what was, at one time, the happiest day of his life. Now all he sees in those wedding photos is the monster that took his daughter's life. The unimaginable anger he has to endure. When he considered that he spent his whole life trying to protect his daughter from this type of evil, only to fail her at the end.

Sadly, many families that find themselves in this surreal reality are certain, that at some point, they will eventually discover a suitable answer which will one day ease their troubled minds. Regrettably, it has been my experience that the world in which we live does not provide this type of peace. It never has, and it never will. This type and all other forms of true peace can only come from being steadfast in one source, Jesus Christ. "Peace I leave with you, my peace I give unto you: not as the world giveth, give I unto you. Let not your heart be troubled, neither let it be afraid." (John 14:27).

You may wonder why I spent so much time weaving this realistic enactment? The answer is three words - “Devil’s in Disguise.” Brothers and sisters hear me and hear me well. As a Blood Born Christian, you will never have a successful mutually beneficial relationship with anyone unless they first have a true relationship with the Son of God, Jesus. Amen. "Be ye not unequally yoked together with unbelievers: for what fellowship hath righteousness with unrighteousness? and what communion hath light with darkness?" (2 Corinthians 6:14). Fortunately, God has not left us in the dark as it relates to spotting these types of Devils. God has provided His Children with spiritual gifts that will protect us and reveal to us the Demons in our presence that would do us great harm. Any Christian can easily test this theory. Our first line of defense is observation. Notice people's behavior when you talk about sports, finance, fashion, or some event that has gone viral. People will join the conversation and remain engaged for hours. But try and shift the conversation toward Jesus, and observe how quickly they seem to lose interest and leave. Such behavior is an indication that two forces are at work. It is either God protecting you from the demon within them or Satan protecting his demon from you. The truth of God will either draw a person into your life or drive a person out of your life. "Suppose ye that I am come to give peace on earth? I tell you, Nay; but rather division: 53 The father shall be divided against the son, and the son against the father; the mother against the daughter, and the daughter against the mother; the mother in law against her daughter in law, and the daughter in law against her mother in law." (Luke 12:51,53).

I know that as lovers of God and His Word, we want everyone to experience the joy we have inside of us. We have the desire to share our Heavenly relationship with others. The Great Commission compels us to do so. But we must remain steadfast and aware of one spiritual guideline. If a person adamantly refuses to hear the good news of Jesus Christ, he is in league with Satan by default. And yes, I know that sounds harsh because many of the unsaved are our family, friends, and neighbors, people we love and care for, but it is true. "For we wrestle not against flesh and blood, but against principalities, against powers, against the rulers of the darkness of this world, against spiritual wickedness in high places." (Ephesians 6:12). The Bible has shown us this type of Demonic possession many times. There are people so entangled with sin that they refuse to hearken unto the voice of the Lord. Consider the crowd at the Crucifixion of our Lord and Savior. There is no way we can know the true size of the crowd for certain. However, some theologians speculate Jerusalem would swell to over a hundred thousand people for the Passover during the time of Christ. It is reasonable to surmise that thousands may have witnessed the Crucifixion of Jesus and heard his last words spoken from the Cross at Calvary. But out of the thousands in attendance, Jesus' last words only convicted two men. The repentant thief that asked Jesus to remember him and the Centurion soldier who some believe also pierced Jesus in the side. "And when the centurion, which stood over against him, saw that he so cried out, and gave up the ghost, he said, Truly this man was the Son of God." (Mark 15:39). If Jesus, the Son of God, could not change everyone he came in contact with, neither will you. Please remember, just as we knowingly follow Christ, others will unknowingly follow Satan. "My sheep hear my voice, and I know them, and they follow me:" (John 10:27).

And yes, I am well aware that I may be repeating the same point, but it bears repeating. Due to the mere fact that Satan has harmed so many Believers and non-believers with deception.

It seems humans are innately drawn to desire or covet that which someone else has, even when they are themselves the envy of others. Men will give little thought to the cost of new desires, which in many cases are not in their best interest. We have all heard those age-old quotes: "if someone jumped off a bridge, the grass is not always greener, lay down with dogs, etc., etc." These adages and attitudes have been around for centuries. God Himself dealt many times with this problem in the Old Testament. God wanted to establish Israel as a Sanctified Nation unto Himself. But the Children of Israel rejected God; they wanted to live and be governed like other Nations. "Then all the elders of Israel gathered themselves together, and came to Samuel unto Ramah,
5 And said unto him, Behold, thou art old, and thy sons walk not in thy ways: now make us a king to judge us like all the nations.
7 And the Lord said unto Samuel, Hearken unto the voice of the people in all that they say unto thee: for they have not rejected thee, but they have rejected me, that I should not reign over them." (1 Samuel 8:4-5,7). "And now, O our God, what shall we say after this? for we have forsaken thy commandments, 11
Which thou hast commanded by thy servants the prophets, saying, The land, unto which ye go to possess it, is an unclean land with the filthiness of the people of the lands, with their abominations, which have filled it from one end to another with their uncleanness. 12 Now therefore give not your daughters unto their sons, neither take their daughters unto your sons, nor seek their peace or their wealth for ever: that ye may be strong, and eat the good of the land, and leave it for an inheritance to your children for ever." (Ezra 9:10-12).

You have read the chapter called Collateral Damage. Scars from past events have been shown to be haunting and long-lasting. After considerable investigation, I am convinced that blindsiding betrayal lies at the core of many cases of Collateral Damage. Consider the origin of Man's current state of existence. Absent our Lord, Humanity resides in a permanent sinful disposition because Adam and Eve betrayed God. The source of that betrayal was a continuation of Satan's Heavenly betrayal. Betrayal is a primary tactic used by Satan. The underlying presence of betrayal is found throughout many events in the Bible. Cain betrayed his brother Abel. "And Cain talked with Abel his brother: and it came to pass, when they were in the field, that Cain rose up against Abel his brother, and slew him." (Genesis 4:8). Jacob betrayed his father Isaac and his brother Esau. "And he said, Thy brother came with subtilty, and hath taken away thy blessing." (Genesis 27:35). Joseph was betrayed by his brothers. "Come, and let us sell him to the Ishmeelites, and let not our hand be upon him; for he is our brother and our flesh. And his brethren were content." (Genesis 37:27). Also, Samson was betrayed by Delilah. "And when Delilah saw that he had told her all his heart, she sent and called for the lords of the Philistines, saying, Come up this once, for he hath shewed me all his heart. Then the lords of the Philistines came up unto her, and brought money in their hand." (Judges 16:18). And the ultimate insult was the betrayal of Jesus by Judas. Consider the irony. God sent His only begotten Son, Jesus, to undue Man's first betrayal. "Now he that betrayed him gave them a sign, saying, Whomsoever I shall kiss, that same is he: hold him fast. 49 And forthwith he came to Jesus, and said, Hail, master; and kissed him." (Matthew 26:48-49). I know these biblical examples of betrayal may seem somewhat extreme to some, but I used them because they have become a part of our collective knowledge. Even the most faithless heathen knows the story of Judas. However, in the average person's daily life, the Devil in Disguise is more covert than Judas, and unlike Jesus, we may find it harder to identify them.

Here is a technique I teach young people; it has helped them detect if they have a friend or foe within their mist. Young lady, if someone asks you to prove your love for them, that is the conduct of a Demonic spirit. And that spirit is trying to lead you down a path toward unrighteousness. Young man, if your friends use terms like mama's boy or I thought you were a man, this behavior is the language used by a Demonic spirit. And those spirits are attempting to lead you also down the path toward unrighteousness. The Demons we face daily do not employ a straight-to-the-juggler-kill method as Cain did with his brother Abel. No, these Demons pretend to be a close confidant; all the while, they administer death by a thousand cuts. They smile in your face and twist a knife in your back. They throw rocks and hide their hands. They seek out the most emotionally vulnerable in our society solely to destroy what little mental stability they have left. Your mother will tell you, "you're going to be a bum because your father was a bum." Your best friend will tell you, "you are not hot enough for a certain type of guy." Society often conveys to us that we do not have sufficient education. We do not possess the right pedigree, or we're from the wrong side of the tracks. They will say you're too old or you do not have enough experience. And how about this one? You're not the right fit. The Devil never stops. We are constantly bombarded with negative proclamations. Which, for the most part, proclaims to you and the rest of the world that there is something wrong with you. The Military has a name for this type of tactic; it is referred to as Psychological Warfare. Satan loves to deploy psychological warfare against us. The Devil knows, if he can win the battle in your mind, he has also won the war for your Soul. "For to be carnally minded is death; but to be spiritually minded is life and peace." (Romans 8:6).

Consider the world in which we live; right has become wrong, and wrong has become right. And if we dare, as true and steadfast Christians, stand on the Word of our God and condemn societies' sinful behavior, we are labeled intolerant or accused of

Hate-mongering. "Woe unto them that call evil good, and good evil; that put darkness for light, and light for darkness; that put bitter for sweet, and sweet for bitter!" (Isaiah 5:20). As believers, our best and only defense against Psychological Warfare is the Word of God. "Wherefore take unto you the whole armour of God, that ye may be able to withstand in the evil day, and having done all, to stand. 14 Stand therefore, having your loins girt about with truth, and having on the breastplate of righteousness; 15 And your feet shod with the preparation of the gospel of peace; 16 Above all, taking the shield of faith, wherewith ye shall be able to quench all the fiery darts of the wicked. 17 And take the helmet of salvation, and the sword of the Spirit, which is the word of God: 18 Praying always with all prayer and supplication in the Spirit, and watching thereunto with all perseverance and supplication for all saints;" (Ephesians 6:13-18).

What is the Armor of God? Glad you asked! We know what armor is, and we know what armor does, but the Armor of God is greater than any known armor Man could ever place upon himself. Just as armor covers a soldier's body for protection, the Blood of Jesus covers the Believer. If we as Christians rest in the full knowledge of who Jesus Christ is and what Christ can do, as well as what Christ has done, we are fully protected. The Bible show's us that the Devil started attacking Jesus while he was yet in his mother's womb. "Now the birth of Jesus Christ was on this wise: When as his mother Mary was espoused to Joseph, before they came together, she was found with child of the Holy Ghost. 19 Then Joseph her husband, being a just man, and not willing to make her a public example, was minded to put her away privily." (Matthew 1:18-19). These attacks on the Christ continue after his birth, eventually ending at the Cross. And not once did Jesus yield any spiritual or physical ground to the attacks of Satan. Steadfast! Jesus never allowed Satan to have any victory over him, and Christ can provide us with the same protection.

"These things I have spoken unto you, that in me ye might have peace. In the world ye shall have tribulation: but be of good cheer; I have overcome the world." (John 16:33).

Let us continue by examining the first piece of the Armor of God. What does it mean to have your Loins Girt About With Truth? Every commander knows it can be a matter of life and death if his soldiers are not composed or secure on the battlefield. The same is true for God's Christian soldiers on the battlefield of life, holding everything in place with the truth of the Word of God. The Christian Church is built upon and stands firm on the solid rock foundation of Jesus Christ. "He saith unto them, But whom say ye that I am? 16 And Simon Peter answered and said, Thou art the Christ, the Son of the living God. 18 And I say also unto thee, That thou art Peter, and upon this rock I will build my church; and the gates of hell shall not prevail against it." (Matthew 16:15-16,18). The truth is vitally important now more so than ever. There is so much misinformation in our society concerning what people believe to be Religion and the god of their understanding. This plays right into Satin's evil hands. He gains power and rules through chaos and confusion. "For God is not the author of confusion, but of peace, as in all churches of the saints." (1 Corinthians 14:33). You need to know that you know. Preach throughout all the world, and proclaim the truth. There is no other way Man can be saved than by the name of Jesus Christ. "Be it known unto you all, and to all the people of Israel, that by the name of Jesus Christ of Nazareth, whom ye crucified, whom God raised from the dead, even by him doth this man stand here before you whole. 12 Neither is there salvation in any other: for there is none other name under heaven given among men, whereby we must be saved." (Acts 4:10,12).

The next piece of the Armor of God is the Breastplate of Righteousness. It is simple in its explanation, but difficult in its application. And, a vital necessity for the Believer's success. You must guard your heart and purge yourself of all unrighteousness to be of any service to our Lord.

This is one of the reasons, if not the main reason Christians are losing in the battle of life. It appears we have too many part-time soldiers fighting in a very real full-time war. A Christian who has not given himself over to righteousness is a spiritual liability. He is a vulnerable soldier on life's battlefield, and Satan can exploit this vulnerability to his advantage. We know the areas in our lives that are not of the Lord, those little embarrassing dark secrets we hide from others. As Christians, we must never forget and always remember; we cannot hide our unrighteousness from a Righteous God. "And ye shall be holy unto me: for I the Lord am holy, and have severed you from other people, that ye should be mine." (Leviticus 20:26).

The third piece of the Armor of God is to Shod your feet with the Preparation of the Gospel of Peace. This is a reference to your daily walk. Are you prepared to offer a Living Word to a dying World? Do you have an unwavering grasp of the gospel of Jesus Christ? Are you evangelizing God's Gospel as you travel life's highways and byways, "Study to shew thyself approved unto God, a workman that needeth not to be ashamed, rightly dividing the word of truth." (2 Timothy 2:15).

The fourth piece of the Armor of God is the Shield of Faith. As a Believer, you know who keeps you and preserves you. A Christian must always rely on God and only God. Our faith lies in Him and only Him, not in ourselves or others. As my Pastor, M.J. Johnson used to say, "Faith is the solid rock in which we stand. All else is seeking sand." A Believer without Faith is not a true and convicted Believer. He will not please God and obtain a good report. "Now faith is the substance of things hoped for, the evidence of things not seen. 2 For by it the elders obtained a good report. 3 Through faith we understand that the worlds were framed by the word of God, so that things which are seen were not made of things which do appear. 4 By faith Abel offered unto God a more excellent sacrifice than Cain, by which he obtained witness that he was righteous, God testifying of his gifts: and by it he being dead yet speaketh. 5 By faith Enoch was translated that he should not see death; and was not found, because God had translated him: for before his translation he had this testimony, that he pleased God. 6 But without faith it is impossible to please him: for he that cometh to God must believe that he is, and that he is a rewarder of them that diligently seek him." (Hebrews 11:1-6).

The fifth piece of the Armor of God is the Helmet of Salvation. A soldier's helmet is the most important piece of his armor. It protects one of the most valuable and vulnerable parts of his body, his head. A headless soldier on the battlefield is a dead soldier on the battlefield. To a true Believer, salvation is our most valued gift, there is nothing greater, and there should be nothing more desirable. "For what shall it profit a man, if he shall gain the whole world, and lose his own soul?" (Mark 8:36). Without salvation, all is lost because there will be no eternal life spent with the Father in Heaven. "For God so loved the world, that he gave his only begotten Son, that whosoever believeth in him should not perish, but have everlasting life." (John 3:16). It is vitally important that we, the true Children of God, convince humanity that without Jesus as their Lord and Savior, they are as dead men that have not yet been laid in their graves. "And he said unto another, Follow me. But he said, Lord, suffer me first to go and bury my father. 60 Jesus said unto him, Let the dead bury their dead: but go thou and preach the kingdom of God." (Luke 9:59-60).

The sixth piece of the Armor of God is the Sword of the Spirit. Every piece of armor before this was designed for defense or protecting the soldier. However, a soldier's sword is a weapon for offense. With his sword, a soldier can use this deadly weapon to defeat his enemy. As Children of God, we also have a deadly weapon: the Word of God. The Word of God is the only thing a true Christian Soldier can use to defeat Satan on the battlefield of life.

"For the word of God is quick, and powerful, and sharper than any twoedged sword, piercing even to the dividing asunder of soul and spirit, and of the joints and marrow, and is a discerner of the thoughts and intents of the heart." (Hebrews 4:12).

In some theological circles, the seventh and final piece of the Armor of God is considered not a piece at all. But, I believe Prayer is a vital piece of the Armor. There are not too many things a soldier in Paul's time would have in common with a soldier in our time. However, there is one thing they do have in common. All soldiers must have and follow their orders. A soldier on a battlefield without orders is similar to a ship without a rudder. He needs to hear from and communicate with his commanders. He needs to know what's the objectives, his rules of engagement, and if there are any tactical advantages present on the battlefield. A Christian Soldier needs to have his orders as well. We receive those orders through the Word of God and by Prayer. Prayer has always been a direct line of communication with our Father in Heaven. We pray for ourselves. We pray for our families and friends. We pray for other Saints on the battlefield. And we pray that the Will of God is fulfilled. "Pray without ceasing. 18 In every thing give thanks: for this is the will of God in Christ Jesus concerning you." (1 Thessalonians 5:17-18).

Since we are on the topic of Soldiers and Battlefields. I want to close this chapter with a housekeeping item. There is a saying in the Military, "No Man shall be left behind." Every Military Commander with any battlefield experience knows there will be war casualties. But soldiers can fight valiantly, knowing their fellow soldiers will risk it all to see them to safety, if they are wounded. Unfortunately, the soldiers in the Army of the Lord do not live by that Creed. I once heard a Pastor say, "the Christian Army is the only Army that kills its wounded." Let me explain. Although we have put on the Whole Armor of God, it is not uncommon for a Christian Soldier to suffer a Wound. A Christian husband may have faltered and had an adulterous relationship.

A Christian woman may have had an abortion. Another Christian may have committed a crime and is going to jail. As long as they sincerely repent, these sins will not negate their Salvation. When a fellow Believer stumbles while on the Path, we should try and offer reassurances of God's Mercy and Love, not condemnation. Please do not add salt to a brother's wounds. "Let us not therefore judge one another any more: but judge this rather, that no man put a stumblingblock or an occasion to fall in his brother's way." (Romans 14:13). Let us not play the role of a Devil in Disguise toward another. You are going to Hell, should never be your default retort for someone who has acknowledged they have made a mistake. I have a saying, "Sin doesn't keep you out, but sinners don't get in." Here's a Biblical example of my point.

"And the scribes and Pharisees brought unto him a woman taken in adultery; and when they had set her in the midst, 4 They say unto him, Master, this woman was taken in adultery, in the very act. 5 Now Moses in the law commanded us, that such should be stoned: but what sayest thou? 6 This they said, tempting him, that they might have to accuse him. But Jesus stooped down, and with his finger wrote on the ground, as though he heard them not. 7 So when they continued asking him, he lifted up himself, and said unto them, He that is without sin among you, let him first cast a stone at her. 8 And again he stooped down, and wrote on the ground. 9 And they which heard it, being convicted by their own conscience, went out one by one, beginning at the eldest, even unto the last: and Jesus was left alone, and the woman standing in the midst. 10 When Jesus had lifted up himself, and saw none but the woman, he said unto her, Woman, where are those thine accusers? hath no man condemned thee? 11 She said, No man, Lord. And Jesus said unto her, Neither do I condemn thee: go, and sin no more." (John 8:3-11)

Chapter Six

THE SPIRIT OF THE MATTER

"But the hour cometh, and now is, when the true worshippers shall worship the Father in spirit and in truth: for the Father seeketh such to worship him." (John 4:23).

This scripture exemplifies why the Bible is called the Living Word. It requires no great stretch of the imagination but rather a spiritual discernment to understand this particular scripture was meant to explain the necessary Christian mindset in today's sinful world. After the events of 2020, we cannot and must not return to the House of God with the same spiritual mindset, which allowed the doors to close in the first place. Once again, this is a poorly veiled reference to those wicked ways mentioned in 2nd Chronicles chapter 7, verse 14. My fellow Believers, we live in critical times. Christians will need every spiritual gift made available by God if we are going to do thus saith the Lord. It is easy to see that people are hurting, many are confused, and most are seeking answers. Now more so than ever before. If you, as a Believer, are not sharing your testimony about the goodness of God and letting your light shine, then you may be the reason someone is testifying about how bad things are getting. "Let your light so shine before men, that they may see your good works, and glorify your Father which is in heaven." (Matthew 5:16).

The gift of Spiritual Discernment has served me well all of my life, and I know it will be a blessing to you as well. If you feel you do not necessarily know how to discern spiritually, I pray that I, along with this book, can help you develop that gift.

"And they shall teach my people the difference between the holy and profane, and cause them to discern between the unclean and the clean." (Ezekiel 44:23). Above all, you must come to the saving knowledge that God is a Spirit. And, if you are going to commune with God, you cannot achieve this in the flesh. It can only be done through the Spirit. "God is a Spirit: and they that worship him must worship him in spirit and in truth." (John 4:24). At the point of your conversion, you received the Holy Ghost. "Then Peter said unto them, Repent, and be baptized every one of you in the name of Jesus Christ for the remission of sins, and ye shall receive the gift of the Holy Ghost." (Acts 2:38).

If you have never experienced the power of the Holy Spirit and you feel you may not have received this gift when you first came to Christ, do not despair there are ways you can know for sure. "He that believeth on me, as the scriptures hath said, out of his belly shall flow rivers of living water." (John 7:38). The Bible shows us in this verse that the evidence of the Holy Spirit within a person shall be made manifest in the righteous Spirit which flows from the person. In other words, are people coming to you thirsting for the things of God and leaving filled with the Word? Although I imagine, if this were your case, you would not have to wonder whether you possess the Holy Spirit - you would know.

The next method used to determine if you possess the Holy Spirit may be controversial. So, let me state here and now that I am not condoning sin. I pray you never sin. However, if you sin and experience overwhelming guilt and shame, these feelings are not from the Devil. You can rest easy for you, my friend, have the Holy Spirit. "My little children, these things write I unto you, that ye sin not. And if any man sin, we have an advocate with the Father, Jesus Christ the righteous:" (1 John 2:1). The feeling you were experiencing was the Holy Spirit convicting and admonishing you because you, a Child of God, sinned. "For whom the Lord loveth he chasteneth, and scourgeth every son whom he receiveth." (Hebrews 12:6).

I am often dumbfounded at how some people in our society are capable of doing any and everything imaginable. Some people's behavior is so morally corrupt that it boggles the righteous mind. And to add insult to injury. They believe they will not have to one day stand before and give an account to a Holy God. "A naughty person, a wicked man, walketh with a froward mouth. 13 He winketh with his eyes, he speaketh with his feet, he teacheth with his fingers; 14 Frowardness is in his heart, he deviseth mischief continually; he soweth discord. 15 Therefore shall his calamity come suddenly; suddenly shall he be broken without remedy." (Proverbs 6:12-15). Also, I am convinced that if people accuse you of judging them, it is because you exemplify the steadfast behavior of someone who possesses the Holy Ghost. And yes, I know Jesus said, "judge not." This is a true and correct statement because many consider man not righteous enough to judge another. "Judge not, that ye be not judged." (Matthew 7:1). However, please bear in mind Jesus said this before the day of Pentecost. Which means the Holy Ghost had not yet arrived. Most people, sinner and saint alike, do not realize it is not the Man judging someone. It is the God within the Man that judges sinful behavior. The judging of the Soul is reserved for Judgment Day by God, but sinful behavior is sinful behavior, and a Believer is not in the wrong when he tells someone the wages of sin is death. If we, the Children of God, do not call sin a sin, who will?

Trust me, one thing I know for certain is that sinners do not condemn other sinners. The thief does not condemn the drug dealer. The drug dealer does not condemn the killer, and the killer does not condemn the rapist. Satan does not work against Satan. Jesus expressed this fact to those who questioned whether his authority was given to him by God. "Then was brought unto him one possessed with a devil, blind, and dumb: and he healed him, insomuch that the blind and dumb both spake and saw. 23 And all the people were amazed, and said, Is not this the son of David? 24 But when the Pharisees heard it, they said, This fellow doth not cast out devils, but by Beelzebub the prince of the devils. 25

And Jesus knew their thoughts, and said unto them, Every kingdom divided against itself is brought to desolation; and every city or house divided against itself shall not stand: 26 And if Satan cast out Satan, he is divided against himself; how shall then his kingdom stand? 27 And if I by Beelzebub cast out devils, by whom do your children cast them out? therefore they shall be your judges. 28 But if I cast out devils by the Spirit of God, then the kingdom of God is come unto you." (Matthew 12:22-28).

And as it was with Jesus in his day, so is it with us now in our day. Satan still uses the same tactics to keep people from hearing or seeing the truth of God. In my experience, the normal response from someone accused of sinning should not be, "you do not have the right to judge me." What should concern them; is the accusing person telling the true. And if they are speaking the truth, be thankful that a merciful God has sent a Saint to help correct your behavior while you yet live. "Wherefore (as the Holy Ghost saith, To day if ye will hear his voice, 8 Harden not your hearts, as in the provocation, in the day of temptation in the wilderness:" (Hebrews 3:7-8). In this case, God has allowed the accused to resolve his or her sins before the Final Judgment. Because on Judgment Day, no one will be allowed to adjudicate their sins. They will only answer for them. After these examples, if you still have doubts about possessing the Holy Ghost, all you need to do at this point is ask God to grant you the imparting of the Holy Spirit. "If ye then, being evil, know how to give good gifts unto your children: how much more shall your heavenly Father give the Holy Spirit to them that ask him?" (Luke 11:13). Now that you are in full possession of the Holy Spirit, what is the next step on your Christian journey? Step one: you must feed and exercise the Spirit Man with the same enthusiasm, if not more, that you have when you feed and exercise the Physical Man. As you know, the physical body has certain needs. It requires food: water, proteins, carbohydrates, and a variety of other nutrients, along with exercise, to operate at its optimal level.

And likewise, the Spiritual Man also has his dietary and exercise requirements, albeit they are somewhat different. "Wherefore laying aside all malice, and all guile, and hypocrisies, and envies, and all evil speakings, 2 As newborn babes, desire the sincere milk of the word, that ye may grow thereby:" (1 Peter 2:1-2). Look at yourself in this fashion and singularity: you are a sealed vessel of God, and you must seek to fill the vessel with nothing but the things of God. "And to know the love of Christ, which passeth knowledge, that ye might be filled with all the fulness of God." (Ephesians 3:19). When you, the vessel of God, are truly filled, it is then and only then, when you will experience the true power of the Holy Spirit. "Verily, verily, I say unto you, He that believeth on me, the works that I do shall he do also; and greater works than these shall he do; because I go unto my Father. 17 Even the Spirit of truth; whom the world cannot receive, because it seeth him not, neither knoweth him: but ye know him; for he dwelleth with you, and shall be in you." (John 14:12,17).

The following is a clear and current example demonstrating why we need the Holy Spirit to provide us with the gift of Spiritual Discernment. It is the summer of 2021, and violent crimes are increasing in America. Many cities have braced themselves as they shattered previous records for violent crimes. The Right, or Republicans, are blaming the Left or Democrats because the Left has defunded some police departments. The Left is blaming the Right because the Republicans have passed legislation allowing people easier access to guns. Both have components rooted in deception and are completely wrong. But when all you are is carnal, and all you see is carnal, and all you hear is carnal, all you will understand is rooted in complete carnality. "They have not known nor understood: for he hath shut their eyes, that they cannot see; and their hearts, that they cannot understand." (Isaiah 44:18). The real reason why crime is on the rise in America is as plain as the nose on your face. After applying discernment and viewing the problem with your spiritual eyes.

The Pandemic closed the Doors of God's House for a year; how could crime not increase? Churches all around America were not opened, and the Bible tells us sin will rise when the righteous are absent. "When the righteous are in authority, the people rejoice: but when the wicked beareth rule, the people mourn. 16 When the wicked are multiplied, transgression increaseth: but the righteous shall see their fall." (Proverbs 29:2,16). Consider what did not happen in the Church during the year 2020. No one was prostrated at the Altar of God pleading for righteousness. No transgressors walked down the aisles of our churches seeking salvation, and lastly, the Baptismal Pools were left completely dry and unused. One can also spiritually discern the long-term side effects that will soon occur due to the closing of God's House. There will be an increase in domestic abuse, drug abuse, alcoholism, depression, and suicides. America has yet to see the full scope of societal decay brought on by the closing of churches across this Country.

As long as Satan keeps those in power blinded to the truth, darkness will continue throughout the land, and the godly solution will be ignored. Here is my Biblical example. "Much people of the Jews therefore knew that he was there: and they came not for Jesus' sake only, but that they might see Lazarus also, whom he had raised from the dead. 10 But the chief priest consulted that they might put Lazarus also to death; 11 Because that by reason of him many of the Jews went away, and believed on Jesus." (John 12:9-11). Let me attempt to explain the absurd circumstances of this scripture. We have here, the Chief Priest in consultation with other religious leaders. These evil men were in charge of God's Temple at the time of Christ. They have decided to murder Jesus, God's Son, because of the miracles he has done and his popularity. Can you see the irony? Just imagine the look on the soldier's face when he received orders from the Chief Priest that Jesus and Lazarus were to be arrested and killed. The Temple leaders had become so spiritually blind that they wanted to kill Jesus for saying he was God's Son and doing God's will.

They also conspired to kill Lazarus as well. However, his crime was not blasphemy. Oh no, Lazarus' crimes were far worst. He had the nerve to die and not stay dead but instead became a living, breathing, walking testament to the power of Jesus.

As you can see, to be spiritually blind can have grave consequences. This is why when a new Convert asks me what's the best way to start reading the Bible. I give specific Spiritual instructions. Allow me to explain; many feel you can start at the beginning of the Bible with Genesis as you would with any other book, but this is completely false. It is difficult to get the full spiritual benefit from the Bible if you attempt to read it in this manner. Take your typical novel; in the beginning, the boy meets the girl. In the middle, the boy loses the girl. And at the very end, the boy finds the girl and they live happily ever after. The Bible is no ordinary book. For example, if you start reading a verse in John, the supporting verse may be found in Genesis. Or, if you discover a question in Revelation, the answer may be found in Daniel. The Bible is God's living, breathing Word; and God is a Spirit. To truly unlock the Bible's full potential and receive clear revelation, you must read it in the Spirit. Thankfully, God has provided us with a way to accomplish this very task, the Holy Ghost. This is one of the many blessings we receive when we are endowed with the Holy Spirit. "But the Comforter, which is the Holy Ghost, whom the Father will send in my name, he shall teach you all things, and bring all things to your remembrance, whatsoever I have said unto you." (John 14:26).

Remember, I hinted to you in chapter 3 Collateral Damage there was a hidden motive in Satan's attack on King David. Although David fought his battles in the physical realm unbeknownst to him, he was a central character on a larger Spiritual Stage. Here is the real reason behind the attack on King David. "For unto us a child is born, unto us a son is given: and the government shall be upon his shoulder: and his name shall be called Wonderful, Counsellor, The mighty God, The everlasting Father,

The prince of Peace. 7 Of the increase of his government and peace there shall be no end, upon the throne of David, and upon his kingdom, to order it, and to establish it with judgment and with justice from henceforth even for ever. The zeal of the Lord of hosts will perform this." (Isaiah 9:6-7). "The book of the generation of Jesus Christ, the son of David, the son of Abraham." (Matthew 1:1). There you have it. Satan knew Jesus had to come through the bloodline of King David. This meant Satan would do everything possible to prevent the Messiah from arriving. This is why he tried to corrupt David and his seed. Satan knew Jesus was going to die for Man. However, he did not know when. Throughout our history the Devil has deployed a shotgun approach with sin. This strategy allows Satan to corrupt as many people as possible, hoping it would stop or delay Christ from coming. "And it repented the Lord that he had made man on the earth, and it grieved him at his heart. 7 And the Lord said, I will destroy man whom I have created from the face of the earth; both man, and beast, and the creeping thing, and the fowls of the air; for it repenteth me that I have made them." (Genesis 6:6-7). Satan no doubt rejoiced after hearing God's declaration. For it appeared that the Devil had finally won the battle against the Creature called Man. The Being that unlike him was created in the likeness and image of the Almighty. Fortunately for us, Satan could not take a victory lap; the Bible tells us it was a short-lived triumph because of Noah. "But Noah found grace in the eyes of the Lord. 9 These are the generations of Noah: Noah was a just man and perfect in his generations, and Noah walked with God." (Genesis 6:8-9).

With your new spiritual mindset, you will have a greater understanding of the Mysteries of God, which are revealed in certain scriptures. "Now to him that is of power to stablish you according to my gospel, and the preaching of Jesus Christ, according to the revelation of the mystery, which was kept secret since the world began, 26 But now is made manifest, and by the scriptures of the prophets, according to the commandment of the everlasting God, made known to all nations for the obedience of faith:" (Romans 16:25-26). Also, with your new ability, your faith in God will increase. And you will see the awesome power of His Word and how those who stand on the Word cannot be defeated. My mother would say, "if God said it, that settles it." The Bible agrees with my mother's statement and conveys it in this manner. "So shall my word be that goeth forth out of my mouth: it shall not return unto me void, but it shall accomplish that which I please, and it shall prosper in the thing whereto I sent it." (Isaiah 55:11).

Let us read the book of Job in the Spirit, I know Job has forty-two chapters. However, the Holy Spirit will reveal to you that God only needed the first eight verses of chapter 1 to prove Satan would not have a victory over Job. "There was a man in the land of Uz, whose name was Job; and that man was perfect and upright, and one that feared God, and eschewed evil. 2 And there were born unto him seven sons and three daughters. 3 His substance also was seven thousand sheep, and three thousand camels, and five hundred yoke of oxen, and five hundred she asses, and a very great household; so that this man was the greatest of all the men of the east. 4 And his sons went and feasted in their houses, every one his day; and sent and called for their three sisters to eat and to drink with them. 5 And it was so, when the days of their feasting were gone about, that Job sent and sanctified them, and rose up early in the morning, and offered burnt offerings according to the number of them all: for Job said, it may be that my sons have sinned, and cursed God in their hearts. Thus did Job continually. 6 Now there was a day when the sons of God came to present themselves before the Lord, and Satan came also among them. 7 And the Lord said unto Satan, Whence comest thou? Then Satan answered the Lord, and said, From going to and fro in the earth, and from walking up and down in it. 8 And the Lord said unto Satan, Hast thou considered my servant Job, that there is none like him in the earth, a perfect and an upright man, one that feareth God, and escheweth evil?" (Job 1:1-8). I love teaching and preaching on Job. You can only imagine how those in attendance are baffled when I tell them the book of Job is simultaneously one of the longest and one of the shortest books in the Bible. I show them the outcome of the entire book in just the first eight verses of chapter 1. Let me explain, look at verse 1; the Bible says Job was perfect and upright. This meant that Job could not be anything but perfect and upright, or the Bible would be wrong. "Thy word is true from the beginning: and every one of thy righteous judgments endureth for ever." (Psalm 119:160). When you read verse 1 and verse 8 in the Spirit, you have all the information about Job you will ever need. On those two verses hinge the entire book of Job as it relates to Job's reaction, response, and final disposition. Verse 8 says God had a conversation with Satan about Job. God said to Satan that there was no man like Job on Earth. He's perfect, righteous, fears God, and avoids evil. Since God is all-knowing, omnipresent, the Alpha and the Omega, in a nutshell, what this meant was Satan could not prevail against Job. Hopefully, you see and understand my point. In chapter 1, verse 8 God said Job was perfect, by default, Job would remain perfect till the last period in chapter 42, no matter what Satan did to him. Remember what my mother said, "If God said it, that settles it." Job was truly perfect because God said he was.

Here is yet another example of a scripture with greater Spiritual meaning. "And the whole earth was of one language, and of one speech. 2 And it came to pass, as they journeyed from the east, that they found a plain in the land of Shinar; and they dwelt there. 3 And they said one to another, Go to, let us make brick, and burn them thoroughly. And they had brick for stone, and slime had they for morter. 4 And they said, Go to, let us build us a city and a tower, whose top may reach unto heaven; and let us make us a name, lest we be scattered abroad upon the face of the whole earth. 5 And the Lord came down to see the city and the tower, which the children of men builded. 6 And the Lord said, Behold, the people is one, and they have all one language;

and this they begin to do: and now nothing will be restrained from them, which they have imagined to do. 7 Go to, let us go down, and there confound their language, that they may not understand one another's speech. 8 So the Lord scattered them abroad from thence upon the face of all the earth: and they left off to build the city." (Genesis 11:1-8). This scripture refers to the blasphemy at the tower of Babel. On the surface, we see the origins of the many different languages mankind currently speaks. However, hidden within these passages are two reprehensible acts. First, when Man attempts to make a name for himself by using the things of God, it is an offense. Heaven is the domain of God, and God decides what will happen there. When Man tries to rule over the things of God, we ultimately will suffer the consequences. "Belshazzar the king made a great feast to a thousand of his lords, and drank wine before the thousand. 3 Then they brought the golden vessels that were taken out of the temple of the house of God which was at Jerusalem; and the king, and his princes, his wives, and his concubines, drank in them. 5 In the same hour came forth fingers of a man's hand, and wrote over against the candlestick upon the plaister of the wall of the king's palace: and the king saw the part of the hand that wrote. 17 Then Daniel answered and said before the king, Let thy gifts be to thyself, and give thy rewards to another; yet I will read the writing unto the king, and make known to him the interpretation. 23 But hast lifted up thyself against the Lord of heaven; and they have brought the vessels of his house before thee, and thou, and thy lords, thy wives, and thy concubines, have drunk wine in them; and thou hast praised the gods of silver, and gold, of brass, iron, wood, and stone, which see not, nor hear, nor know: and the God in whose hand thy breath is, and whose are all thy ways, hast thou not glorified: 30 In that night was Belshazzar the king of the Chaldeans slain." (Daniel 5:1,3,5,17,23,30).

The next and most dangerous offense in this plan of Man, was in direct opposition to God's plan of Salvation. God drove Man out of the Garden of Eden because of Adam and Eve's sins.

The Garden was a model of Heaven on Earth. God decided the only way Man could ever enter Heaven again was when Man was absent of sin. And the only way a sinner could accomplish this is through God's Son, Jesus. "Jesus saith unto him, I am the way, the truth, and the life: no man cometh unto the Father, but by me." (John 14:6). I know our intellect tells us that there is no possible way Man could have ever built a tower to Heaven. But, remember what God said in verse 6, "and now nothing will be restrained from them, which they have imagined to do." Do you believe God would have troubled himself over a tall building? If that were the case, he would have stopped the building of the Sears Tower. God's Word and actions prove that Man could have very well accomplished their goal. Can you imagine the many frightening possibilities if humanity was of one mind and in league with Satan? The ramifications of such power would be unspeakable. This should be of no surprise to Christians; the Bible tells us of the supernatural abilities we could have if we only had enough faith. "And the Lord said, If ye had faith as a grain of mustard seed, ye might say unto this sycamine tree, Be thou plucked up by the root, and be thou planted in the sea; and it should obey you." (Luke 17:6). The Children of God must always consider the Spirit of the matter, for God has little regard toward the flesh. So, it is unfortunate that most of our concerns, as Christians, have shown to be fleshly. "And I say unto you my friends, Be not afraid of them that kill the body, and after that have no more that they can do. 5 But I will forewarn you whom ye shall fear: Fear him, which after he hath killed hath power to cast into hell; yea, I say unto you, Fear him." (Luke 12:4-5).

There is a great deal of controversy surrounding the Coronavirus Vaccine. Many Believers and non-believers alike think this is a trick of the enemy to get them to accept a hidden microchip. Some Christians believe this is a way Satan can get them to accept what would actually be the Mark of the Beast. While others believe it may be some form of population control.

Where is your faith? Do you believe the God you serve would allow you to fall victim to such a scheme? Do you honestly think God, your Heavenly Father, who's love for you goes beyond all measures, would deny you access to Heaven because His Child was unknowingly duped? That type of behavior is not indicative of the Just God we serve. So, what should we as Believers do about this matter? The answer is simple, look up and live. As Believers, we must stop looking down at sinful men and the many obstacles they will set in our path. Always look to God, who is greater. "The Lord is my shepherd; I shall not want. 2 He maketh me to lie down in green pastures: he leadeth me beside the still waters. 3 He restoreth my soul: he leadeth me in the paths of righteousness for his name's sake. 4 Yea, though I walk through the valley of the shadow of death, I will fear no evil: for thou art with me; thy rod and thy staff they comfort me. 5 Thou preparest a table before me in the presence of mine enemies: thou anointest my head with oil; my cup runneth over. 6 Surely goodness and mercy shall follow me all the days of my life: and I will dwell in the house of the Lord for ever." (Psalm 23:1-6).

I fully understand that we are in the last days. And I know Satan will perform all types of heinous evils. The Bible tells us this. "And he had power to give life unto the image of the beast, that the image of the beast should both speak, and cause that as many as would not worship the image of the beast should be killed. 16 And he causeth all, both small and great, rich and poor, free and bond, to receive a mark in their right hand, or in their foreheads:" (Revelation 13:15-16). First and foremost, there has to be a real Beast. And if you believe he is here and hidden, then please rely on the Holy Spirit to interpret these scriptures. In verse 15 of Revelation chapter 13, the Beast required worship. And those that did not worship him were put to death. This means the diverse multitude that remained in verse 16 were those who worshiped the Beast and freely took his Mark. Also, the vaccine cannot deliver the Mark of the Beast if the Bible is the Word of Truth. Remember, verse 16 states the Mark will be placed in your right hand or upon your forehead. The Covid-19 Vaccine is administered as a shot to the left or right shoulder, not in your right hand or forehead. Let's say, for the sake of argument. The Devil weaponized the Vaccine as a way to harm those of us who serve the Lord. Even if this was the case, the Bible tells us Satan would not have great success with such an evil scheme. "In righteousness shalt thou be established: thou shalt be far from oppression; for thou shalt not fear: and from terror; for it shall not come near thee. 17 No weapon that is formed against thee shall prosper; and every tongue that shall rise against thee in judgment thou shalt condemn. This is the heritage of the servants of the Lord, and their righteousness is of me, saith the Lord." (Isaiah 54:14,17).

Since we have segued into the subject of Satan harming Believers by way of our bodies or health, let me address this matter a little more. The examples I presented earlier were mostly external applications for the power of the Holy Spirit (i.e., spiritual discernment and interpretation). However, if you apply supernatural faith, the Holy Spirit can also be used internally. The Bible tells us that Jesus cleansed the Temple of God when he found corruption. This act was important because it appears in all four gospels. "And Jesus went into the temple of God, and cast out all them that sold and bought in the temple, and overthrew the tables of the moneychangers, and the seats of them that sold doves, 13 And said unto them, It is written, My house shall be called the house of prayer; but ye have made it a den of thieves. 14 And the blind and the lame came to him in the temple; and he healed them." (Matthew 21:12-14). Before Jesus was crucified, God resided in the Temple when He fellowshipped with Man on Earth. The Temple was to remain Holy, for God is Holy. "And let them make me a sanctuary; that I may dwell among them." (Exodus 25:8). As Believers, we know we are the Temple of the living God. Just as Jesus removed the things that defiled the Temple during his time, the Holy Spirit will remove the things that now defile the Temple. In case you were wondering what are the things that defile us, the New Temple besides sin. Here are some examples: sickness, disease, depression, and despair. Let me be clear. I am not telling you to stop seeing your Doctor or Therapist, or stop taking your Medication. What I am telling you, through the power of the Holy Spirit, your Doctor or Therapist will tell you to stop taking your Medication, because you are now healed. Notice what took place inside the Temple once Jesus cleansed it; verse 14 of Matthew chapter 21 says Jesus healed the sick. Here's how I pray concerning this matter. "Father, I am in you, and you are in me. If you see anything in me that is not of you, please remove it: cancer is not of you, diabetes is not of you, high blood pressure is not of you, in Jesus' name I pray, Amen." Faith is the key and not your typical ordinary faith; this requires supernatural faith combined with praying and fasting. "Then came the disciples to Jesus apart, and said, Why could not we cast him out? 20 And Jesus said unto them, Because of your unbelief: for verily I say unto you, If ye have faith as a grain of mustard seed, ye shall say unto this mountain, Remove hence to yonder place; and it shall remove; and nothing shall be impossible unto you. 21 Howbeit this kind goeth not out but by prayer and fasting." (Matthew 17:19-21).

I cannot begin to imagine how disappointed God must feel when His Children put down the spiritual gifts He has given us. And instead, choose to fight our enemy, the Devil behaving like the Devil. Always remember, this is Spiritual Warfare. My mother instilled this knowledge into me many years ago. Let me explain; I once owned a fast-food franchise. My mother, along with another employee, was working the late-night shift. It was now closing time. While my mother and the other employee were locking up, a young man came in with a gun, fully attending to rob the restaurant. Little did he know that Jesus was also working the late shift that night. My mother did not follow the restaurant's safety protocols. She did not trigger the silent alarm or grab a knife or a gun. Instead, she chose to do something completely different.

She turned it over to Jesus, by praising the Lord. My mother took the other employee by the hand, and they both walked out of the restaurant, singing what a friend we have in Jesus. Here's my proof that God honors His Word. My mother and the employee were not harmed, and the would-be robber changed his mind and left empty-handed. "The name of the Lord is a strong tower: the righteous runneth into it, and is safe." (Proverbs 18:10). What I learned from my mother's experience, was, we cannot beat the Devil at his own game. We cannot outshoot the Devil. We cannot out lie the Devil. And we definitely cannot out-curse the Devil. Christians are at their strongest when they are on their knees, getting spiritual help. "(For the weapons of our warfare are not carnal, but mighty through God to the pulling down of strong holds;)" (2 Corinthians 10:4).

Let me leave you with this. In life, never give any credence to the Flesh. You must always examine the Heart, scratch the surface and peer behind the curtain. Are some of the battles you are currently fighting due solely to you and your actions? Or are you similar to King David, and Satan is attacking you and yours because he knows greatness is coming in your line? If friends and family are unfairly mistreating you. Remember, it is not them you are fighting; it is Satan.

"Then entered Satan into Judas surnamed Iscariot, being of the number of the twelve:" (Luke 22:3).

Chapter Seven

THE POWER OF THE TONGUE

"Death and life are in the power of the tongue: and they that love it shall eat the fruit thereof." (Proverbs 18:21).

This is one of the most misunderstood verses in the Bible. Many Christians read this passage and believe they can speak Physical death into someone's life. Nothing could be farther from the truth. However, and I am aware this may sound like I am contradicting myself. Yes, we can speak life into a person's existence. But only if they are willing to hear. As for speaking death, it is a lot more complicated, and it is not how most imagine this power. It is how God designed it because it only concerns Eternal death. Always remember, our God is a Spirit, and His concerns towards us are mainly Spiritual. "And the Lord said, My spirit shall not always strive with man, for that he also is flesh: yet his days shall be an hundred and twenty year." (Genesis 6:3). Here's how a Christian can speak life and death with their tongue. While studying the Bible, I discovered three forms of death. The first form of death is the form we are all aware of. It is Physical death. "Then said Jesus unto them plainly, Lazarus is dead." (John 11:14). The second form of death is called the Second death or Eternal death. This is the one you have a say over. You must decide if you will spend Eternity in the smoking or non-smoking section. "But the fearful, and unbelieving, and the abominable, and murderers, and whoremongers, and sorcerers, and idolaters, and all liars, shall have their part in the lake which burneth with fire and brimstone: which is the second death." (Revelation 21:8). The third form of death is more complicated. It is Spiritual death. This is the death Adam and Eve suffered immediately after they ate from the Tree of Knowledge. It is also the same death humanity inherited from Adam, not to mention Physical death. "For as in Adam all die, even so in Christ shall all be made alive." (1 Corinthians 15:22). Spiritual death separates Man from God. "And the Lord God said, Behold, the man is become as one of us, to know good and evil: and now, lest he put forth his hand, and take also of the tree of life, and eat, and live for ever: 24 So he drove out the man; and he placed at the east of the garden of Eden Cherubims, and a flaming sword which turned every way, to keep the way of the tree of life." (Genesis 3:22,24).

Can you imagine what this world would become if we were truly endowed with the power to speak Physical death upon our fellow man? Our cities would look like a war zone. Corpses would line the streets of every town and every community in America. Allow me to paint a picture of your average Monday. It is Monday morning, and you just killed a telemarketer in India because he woke you an hour early. Unfortunately for him, you were not interested in changing your healthcare provider. Also, you will be delayed as you drive into the office because the expressway is a cemetery. Remember, you are not the only one gifted with the power to speak life or death. And, congratulation on your recent promotion. Your boss met his early demise when he pointed out this was the third time this week you were late. However, here's some advice, I would not get too comfortable in this your new position of authority if I were you. You have an afternoon meeting scheduled with your department heads, and the first topic on the agenda is job cuts. I trust you see my point regarding the power of the tongue.

God wants us to speak blessings into people's lives, not curses. Satan does not need any help from us when it comes to spewing vileness into the lives of our fellow man. Consider how toxic the Internet has become. "The wicked is snared by the transgression of his lips: but the just shall come out of trouble." (Proverbs 12:13). "For by thy words thou shalt be justified, and by thy words thou shalt be condemned." (Matthew 12:37).

As these scriptures state there is power in your tongue or the words that you speak. You are the one that speaks life or death into your existence, not others. "And one of the malefactors which were hanged railed on him, saying, if thou be Christ, save thyself and us. 40 But the other answering rebuked him, saying, Dost not thou fear God, seeing thou art in the same condemnation? 41 And we indeed justly; for we receive the due reward of our deeds: but this man hath done nothing amiss. 42 And he said unto Jesus, Lord, remember me when thou comest into thy kingdom. 43 And Jesus said unto him, Verily I say unto thee, Today shalt thou be with me in paradise." (Luke 23:39-43). At the Crucifixion of Jesus, one thief did not believe Jesus was the Christ. He used his tongue to speak death upon his Eternal Soul by questioning Jesus' identity. This spiritually blind evil thief used similar language at the end of Jesus' earthly life as Satan used at the beginning of Jesus' earthly ministry. "And the devil said unto him, if thou be the the Son of God, command this stone that it be made bread." (Luke 4:3). The bible states there was another thief crucified with Jesus at Calvary. Unlike the evil thief, this man was repentant. He used his tongue to speak life upon his Eternal Soul by choosing to defend and believe in Jesus. And with his confession came his Salvation. "For whosoever will save his life shall lose it: and whosoever will lose his life for my sake shall find it." (Matthew 16:25).

Throughout the Gospels, Jesus would make statements that left many baffled, including his Disciples. One such statement was, "He that hath ears to hear, let him hear." This statement usually followed a spiritually profound message. And unfortunately for most, they could not comprehend the message because they were spiritually dead. "Salt is good: but if the salt have lost his savour, wherewith shall it be seasoned? 35 It is neither fit for the land, nor yet for the dunghill; but men cast it out. He that hath ears to hear, let him hear." (Luke 14:34-35). The true followers of Christ had to listen to his messages with their Spiritual Ears. Because Jesus, being in the Spirit, spoke with a Spiritual Tongue. The new revelation blessed those who heard his message with their Spiritual Ear. A Believer speaks life and encouragement to others when God uses their tongue spiritually to speak a word of revelation. The individual who hears your statement with his Spiritual Ears. Instantly knows he has heard from God because it resonated in his Spirit. This works both ways, stand ready to hear from God no matter who is speaking and regardless of the circumstances. God will speak and teach at any time and any place. This is what separated and saved the one thief that hung on the Cross next to Jesus. He knew on that fateful day at Calvary that the hand of God was at work. As Children of God we must allow the Holy Spirit to use our tongues to speak about the good news of Jesus Christ. Then it is contingent upon that person to hear the truth of our Lord and live. This is accomplished when the person accepts Jesus into their life. "He that hath the Son hath life; and he that hath not the Son of God hath not life." (1 John 5:12).

The unrighteous speak death with their tongues in two ways. First, when they tell themselves and others there is no God. Those that choose to believe this lie are truly dead men walking. "But the tongue can no man tame; it is an unruly evil, full of deadly poison." (James 3:8). Second, when men believe God exists, but they choose to hear and live by their own words and not God's. Case in point, I often hear divorced middle age men saying they will never marry again. They also admit that they will not abstain from sex. They have decided to live absent a wife but not absent sexual relationships. These men have chosen to become Reprobates and ignore God's Word, this can be deadly. "Examine yourselves, whether ye be in the faith; prove your own selves. Know ye not your own selves, how that Jesus Christ is in you, except ye be reprobates?" (2 Corinthians 13:5).

Thus far no natural Man of his own accord has escaped the Physical and Spiritual death brought into the world by our father, Adam. Nonetheless, by the power of their tongue, all Men can escape the fiery Eternal death that was originally imposed upon Satan and the fallen angels. "That if thou shall confess with thy mouth the Lord Jesus, and shalt believe in thine heart that God hath raised him from the dead, thou shalt be saved. 10 For with the heart man believeth unto righteousness; and with the mouth confession is made unto salvation." (Romans 10:9-10). We can escape the awful horrors of Eternal death by confessing with our tongues Jesus Christ is Lord and become Born Again. "Jesus answered and said unto him, Verily, verily, I say unto thee, Except a man be born again, he cannot see the kingdom of God." (John 3:3). We must take every precaution to restrain our tongue. We must choose our words wisely because we never know who is listening. The day we stumble in the flesh and curse someone out at work; may have been the day the new guy was going to ask you about Jesus. "Wherefore, my beloved brethren, let every man be swift to hear, slow to speak, slow to wrath:" (James 1:19).

We must make every effort to protect our reputation and integrity. We must never forget that we are God's representatives here on Earth. Once while teaching the disciples what to expect at the time of his departure. One of the disciples asked Jesus to show them his Father. “Philip saith unto him, Lord, show us the Father, and it sufficeth us. 9 Jesus saith unto him, Have I been so long time with you, and yet hast thou not known me, Philip? he that hath seen me hath seen the Father; and how sayest thou then, Show us the Father? 10 Believest thou not that I am in the Father, and the Father in me? the words that I speak unto you I speak not of myself: but the Father that dwelleth in me, he doeth the works." (John 14:8-10). Just as it was in the time of Jesus, it is now in our present time. People want answers. They want to see and hear from the Father. Several years ago, there was a Religious movement that asked the question, “What Would Jesus Do?”. I am not knocking this movement because it brought many non-believers into the Faith. However, as a pure Child of God, I believe there exists another way to phrase the question. Which is, What Would You Do? "Let this mind be in you, which was also in Christ Jesus: 6 Who, being in the form of God, thought it not robbery to be equal with God:" (Philippians 2:5-6). We rob ourselves and others of the many blessings we have at the ready from God when we deny or do not access the power we have in us through Christ Jesus.

Currently, medical science has not completely cured anyone of the disease known as Diabetes. Yet there does exist a cure for Diabetes and all other types of diseases. "And Jesus went about all the cities and villages, teaching in their synagogues, and preaching the gospel of the kingdom, and healing every sickness and every disease among the people." (Matthew 9:35). As this scripture states, Jesus healed all types of diseases and sicknesses. Jesus possessed the power to heal, which means we also have the power to heal. "Verily, verily, I say unto you, He that believeth on me, the works that I do shall he do also; and greater works than these shall he do; because I go unto my Father." (John 14:12).

As I said earlier, we rob ourselves, when we do not access the power we receive from God to do His Will. We have to ask ourselves, is it robbery or theft? All signs point to theft. Satan has stolen our birthright. We are Children of God and were created to rule here on Earth by the power of God. Satan has used the same tricks and deception to steal our birthrights and blessings as Jacob used on his brother Esau and Isaac, his father. "And he said, Is not he rightly named Jacob? for he hath supplanted me these two times: he took away my birthright; and, behold, now he hath taken away my blessing. And he said, Hast thou not reserved a blessing for me?" (Genesis 27:36). I have asked this question and am now asking it again. How do we not know who we are and lack any power we should possess? One reason is Psychological Warfare from chapter 5, The Devil in Disguise.

Do not be alarmed. This is not a continuation of that chapter; we are still studying The Power of The Tongue. However, we are now looking at the many uses of the tongue. Consider this an Psychological overview of what is said and how it is said. The Devil has perpetrated upon us the worst kind of Psychological Warfare, a form of Brainwashing. I know the term brainwashing may trouble some readers; nevertheless, it seems true, and the scriptures support this theory. "In whom the god of this world hath blinded the minds of them which believe not, lest the light of the glorious gospel of Christ, who is the image of God, should shine unto them." (2 Corinthians 4:4). A blinded mind is a mind that Satan has clearly tampered with, and that is the definition of brainwashing. What else would you call it when a Believer does not truly follow the God he says he serves?

Satan has robbed us or caused Christians to forget their true identity. He attempted to use this tactic on Jesus. "And the devil said unto him, If thou be the Son of God, command this stone that it be made bread." (Luke 4:3). Satan tried to get Jesus to follow his commands by calling into question Jesus' identity. Are you the Son of God? If Jesus had done what Satan had asked, all would have been lost. Please do not take this lightly; how we identify ourselves is vital to our success on the battlefield of life. If Satan can call into question our identity, he can sow doubt and discord. If we do not know our true name, we do not know who we are. And if we do not know who we are, we are unaware of all the rights and privileges associated with our true identity. Here is my point, Jesus and the Apostles called their followers the Children of God. "Blessed are the peacemakers: for they shall be called the children of God." (Matthew 5:9). "For ye are all the children of God by faith in Christ Jesus." (Galatians 3:26). "The Spirit itself beareth witness with our spirit, that we are the children of God: 17 And if children, then heirs; heirs of God, and joint-heirs with Christ; if so be that we suffer with him, that we may be also glorified together." (Romans 8:16-17).

At some point in the history of the Faith, we moved away from calling ourselves the Children of God. And we began referring to ourselves as Christians. The term Christian appears only three times in the King James Bible. Twice in the book of Acts and once in 1st Peter. "Then departed Barnabas to Tarsus, for to seek Saul: 26 And when he had found him, he brought him unto Antioch. And it came to pass, that a whole year they assembled themselves with the church, and taught much people. And the disciples were called Christians first in Antioch." (Acts 11:25-26). In the early days of the Church, followers of Jesus were called every evil thing under the sun by non-believers. They said we practiced incest because we refer to each other as brother and sister. They also believed the followers of Jesus were cannibals. Because they ate of the Lord's body when they participated in the Sacrament. And the Bible states that during that period, they started calling the followers of Christ Christians in the Syrian city of Antioch. The term was not considered a compliment at the time. No, they meant it as an insult. But, over time, followers of Christ embraced the title, and eventually, Christian became the recognizable name for those who traveled the path.

I believe embracing the title Christian led us to a state of weakness and a lack of faith which plagues the Church currently. I am not suggesting we completely abandon the term entirely. I have used the term Christian many times in this very book. Nonetheless, there is a difference between a title and a name. And depending on the situation, those differences can cause people to react and respond differently. For example, one of the largest Car companies in America is the Ford Motor Corporation. Some of the descendants of the founder Henry Ford have held several different titles in that Corporation, including CEO. However, the titles are given or taken away based on the decisions of the shareholders or by Ford's Board of Directors. But neither the shareholders nor the Board of Directors can vote to take away the name Ford or the inheritance and benefits that the name has provided the children of Henry Ford for over a century. This example makes it clear that the power is held in the name and not the title. Here is my biblical example, this passage shows a difference between a title like Chief of Priests and the name of Jesus or Paul. "And God wrought special miracles by the hands of Paul: 12 So that from his body were brought unto the sick handkerchiefs or aprons, and the diseases departed from them, and the evil spirits went out of them. 13 Then certain of the vagabond Jews, exorcists, took upon them to call over them which had evil spirits the name of the Lord Jesus, saying, We adjure you by Jesus whom Paul preacheth. 14 And there were seven sons of one Sceva, a Jew, and chief of the priests, which did so. 15 And the evil spirit answered and said, Jesus I know, and Paul I know; but who are ye? 16 And the man in whom the evil spirit was leaped on them, and overcame them, and prevailed against them, so that they fled out of that house naked and wounded." (Acts 19:11-16). This scripture proves there is power in the name. The evil spirits knew and responded to the authority of Paul and the name of Jesus. That was not the case with those attempting to use the power of a title.

We have all seen the motivational signs people have hanging in their homes and office. Statements that point out how special and unique they are and what they can accomplish if they believe in themselves. Everyone knows that there is power in positive thinking and positive speaking. These actions have motivated some in our society to reach heights in business, entertainment, and science that boggles the mind. Outstanding achievements should also be the case in the Faith base community. The World should marvel at the numerous wonders that God's Children have accomplished. "And all nations shall call you blessed: for ye shall be a delightsome land, saith the Lord of hosts." (Malachi 3:12). It is my belief that had we not appropriated the title Christian but held to the Biblical designation of Child of God. The Faith would be more Spiritually Minded and less Carnal.

Once again, I am not saying we should no longer answer to the name Christian. What I am saying. Those who truly follow Christ and hold to the title of Christian must preach, teach, and understand that our faith in Christ and the love God has for us is based on relationship. Terms such as Child of God or Son of God denote a relationship. We must be sincere and true to ourselves to defeat Satan and his Psychological Mind games. We must know who we are and who's we are. Are your words and actions the acts of a Child of God?

During the average day, your tongue is used by you, Satan, or God. It is incumbent upon you to know who is doing the majority of the talking. Do people hear and see the Father when they see and hear you? Many will consider my remarks about the name Christian as trivial. But in this case, the Devil is in the details. Satan will attack what most believe are little insignificant points of interest. Had Jesus turned an insignificant stone into bread, he would not have succeeded in dying for our sins on the Cross. Had the three Hebrew boys eaten from the King's table, they would have perished in the Fiery Furnace. "But Daniel purposed in his heart that he would not defile himself with the portion of the king's meat, nor with the wine which he drank: therefore he requested of the prince of the eunuchs that he might not defile himself. 12 Prove thy servants, I beseech thee, ten days; and let them give us pulse to eat, and water to drink." (Daniel 1:8,12). "But if not, be it known unto thee, O king, that we will not serve thy gods, nor worship the golden image which thou has set up. 23 And these three men, Shadrach, Meshach, and Abednego, fell down bound into the midst of the burning fiery furnace. 25 He answer and said, Lo, I see four men loose, walking in the midst of the fire, and they have no hurt; and the form of the fourth is like the Son of God." (Daniel 3:18,23,25). As you can see, what may appear insignificant or trivial to some. Satan can use that to cause us great harm down the road. Especially so, if you lack insight, or spiritual discernment.

In conclusion, History has shown that some of the most heinous acts of evil perpetrated on Humanity were committed by people calling themselves Christians. Members of the Ku Klux Klan consider themselves Christians and believe they are doing the will and work of God. My brothers and sisters, we must speak life and live as Christian Children of God. Here's how we can view the term Christian. Every Child of God can be called a Christian but not every Christian can be called a Child of God.

"Ye shall know them by their fruits. Do men gather grapes of thorns, or figs of thistles? 17 Even so every good tree bringeth forth good fruit; but a corrupt tree bringeth forth evil fruit. 18 A good tree cannot bring forth evil fruit, neither can a corrupt tree bring forth good fruit." (Matthew 7:16-18).

Chapter Eight

JESUS OR ADAM NOT BOTH

"And the Lord God called unto Adam, and said unto him, Where art thou?" (Genesis 3:9) "And she shall bring forth a son, and thou shalt call his name Jesus: for he shall save his people from their sins." (Matthew 1:21).

First and foremost, without a shadow of doubt, let me state that the Gift God gave us in His Son, Jesus Christ, far outweighs that which was lost to us the moment Adam sinned. "Not by works of righteousness which we have done, but according to his mercy he saved us, by the washing of regeneration, and renewing of the Holy Ghost; 6 Which he shed on us abundantly through Jesus Christ our Saviour; 7 That being justified by his grace, we should be made heirs according to the hope of eternal life." (Titus 3:5-7).

When I visit my primary care Doctor for an illness or a physical, my Physician will ask me a series of questions. What I find odd is that the questions are not necessarily about me. They seem to be more about my parents and grandparent's health and cause of death. The physician would ask questions such as: is there a history of heart disease or high blood pressure in your family? Are your parents still alive, and if not, what was their cause of death? He may also ask what was the cause of death for your grandparents. I soon discovered the purpose for this noninvasive procedure was to diagnose my Genetic Predisposition for certain diseases. Genetic Predisposition is a fancy way to say Papa and Nana may have made me sick. This brought me to an interesting question. Have I passed on anything detrimental to my children?

The greatest experience of my life was when I became a father. Watching my children grow from toddlers to adolescents has been enjoyable and enlightening. However, I began to observe certain behavioral traits that were uniquely me. This was not a learned behavior they developed because they observed me do something. No! This was something much deeper. Somehow my children had begun to display aspects of my secret childhood behavior. Unknown behavior they never had the opportunity to observe, yet by some unforeseen force, it was passed down to them. To protect the innocent, I will not disclose what type of behavior my children were displaying. Let's just say, I was both shocked and perplexed. However, what I will disclose, is this experience has given me greater insight into Original sin or the sin passed down through our bloodline from our father, Adam.

One of the shortest verses in the Bible is "Jesus wept." (John 11:35). There is not a consensus among Theologians on why Jesus cried at the graveside of Lazarus. After all, Jesus knew before he arrived that he would raise Lazarus from the dead. So, why cry for a man that would be alive again shortly? "These things said he: and after that he saith unto them, Our friend Lazarus sleepeth; but I go, that I may awake him out of sleep." (John 11:11). There had to exist a hidden reason why Jesus became so overwhelmed with emotions. Some Theologians believe Jesus wept because he felt the pain of those around him grieving the loss of Lazarus. Many of you have experienced this kind of emotional pain in your life; I also have felt empathetic toward another person's suffering. I remember taking my baby daughter in for a series of shots. As you can imagine, she was not all too happy about this necessary but painful event in her young life. Understandably, after it was over, my little girl was left in tears due to the physical and emotional trauma of the experience. My daughter looked up at me with a confused expression on her little face. Above all else, I was her father, the man she thought would protect her and keep her from all harm.

With tears streaming down her cheeks, she asked me one simple question, which shook me to my core. Why? And that one little word reduced me, a full-grown man, to tears. Naturally, the nurse in attendance was baffled by my behavior. Her response was, I understand why your daughter is crying; but I don't understand why you are crying. I replied, it hurts me more than it hurts her.

A second school of thought believes that Jesus wept at the grave of Lazarus because it troubled him to see the current state of the Children of Israel. No doubt, it caused Jesus to wonder how have God's beloved Children become so thoroughly blinded by the Devil. How could they not understand the feelings God had toward them? "For God so loved the world, that he gave his only begotten Son, that whosoever believeth in him should not perish, but have everlasting life." (John 3:16). At this point in his Ministry, Jesus had undergone a great deal. "He came unto his own, and his own received him not." (John 1:11). Also, while traveling the path God had predestined for him, many of Jesus' followers abandoned him and his cause. "From that time many of his disciples went back, and walked no more with him." (John 6:66). The Children of Israel had become so beguiled by Satan they could not see Jesus for who he was. This vexed Jesus to the depth of his spirit. "Now Jesus was not yet come into the town, but was in that place where Martha met him. 31 The Jews then which were with her in the house, and comforted her, when they saw Mary, that she rose up hastily and went out, followed her, saying, She goeth unto the grave to weep there. 32 Then when Mary was come where Jesus was, and saw him, she fell down at his feet, saying unto him, Lord, if thou hadst been here, my brother had not died. 33 When Jesus therefore saw her weeping, and the Jews also weeping which came with her, he groaned in the spirit, and was trouble. 34 And said, Where have ye laid him? They said unto him, Lord, come and see." (John 11:30-34). I believe this is why the Master wept, for he saw and experienced firsthand how far Adam's seed had fallen away from God.

A familiar example may help you better understand how Adam's sins were passed to us, his offspring. If you look at sin as you would a Virus, it becomes easier for us to understand how it's passed from one person to another. Let us use the fictitious Zombie Virus as my example for sin. We have all seen enough horror movies about zombies to know zombies have one purpose and one purpose only, which is to feed. And because he seeks to gratify that one need, a zombie spreads the virus everywhere he goes, creating more and more zombies. This is the premise of every movie about zombies. They roam from place to place, seeking their next victim. If one zombie enters a farmhouse with two people present in the house, eventually, three zombies will emerge from that house. Those three will then create six, and those six will create twelve, and so on; in due course, there are only a few humans left living.

A sinner's behavior is remarkably similar to that of a zombie. A sinner's singular goal is self-gratification, whatever that may be, sex, drugs, alcohol, greed, revenge, etc. A sinner moves from place to place, person to person, house to house, school to school, job to job, and unfortunately, church to church, seeking to fulfill his or her needs. And because of this carnality, sin will spread throughout the land. Husbands have infected their wives, and wives have infected their husbands. Fathers have infected their sons, and mothers have infected their daughters. Children have infected their friends, loved ones have infected loved ones, and so on. Please give this some consideration. Was the guy or girl with whom you lost your virginity an enemy? Or was it someone you thought loved you? Was the person who gave you your first hit of weed a friend or a foe? Are you a womanizer because your father too was a womanizer? Do you resent men because your mother had a deep resentment for men? Sin is so infectious that it does not require any relationship between individuals to defile all to their core. For example, I once saw evil jump from one car on the highway to another. A guy was driving somewhat erratic on his commute home.

By his aggressive behavior, you could easily see he was angry at someone or something. This distracted and reckless driver cut off another motorist, almost causing an accident. Instead of praising God for the miracle of being saved from an accident, the motorist who was nearly hit got angry and started chasing and yelling obscenities at the reckless driver. I think you see my point. Sin is a virus, and it has sickened all of us to the brink of despair, but fortunately for the Children of Adam, Jesus Christ is the cure for this sin sickness.

Recently I was home watching television one weekend morning. A commercial interrupted my program, as we all know will happen. It was an advertisement for a fast-food restaurant. The commercial's premise was that everything is better with bacon on it. While that statement may or may not be true, I must admit that I do like bacon on many things and if I am being honest. I like bacon just by itself. Nevertheless, others would beg to differ, which makes the bacon statement debatable. However, one thing I know to be true without debate is that everything is better with Jesus in the midst. "The thief cometh not, but for to steal, and to kill, and to destroy: I am come that they might have life, and that they might have it more abundantly." (John10:10). And yes, I can hear detractors say that my statement about Jesus is debatable also. And here is my response to those who would dare disagree with the statement. No one! Man, woman, or child who has sincerely accepted Jesus Christ as their Lord and Savior could or would tell you they regret having the Lord in their life. "Then said Jesus unto the twelve, Will ye also go away? 68 Then Simon Peter answered him, Lord, to whom shall we go? thou hast the words of eternal life. 69 And we believe and are sure that thou art that Christ, the Son of the living God." (John 6:67-69). Throughout my life. I have observed and interacted with countless numbers of people from around the world. In my observations, I have noticed a recognizable difference in the behavior of people who profess Christ and those who do not. The behavior of people who are not saved are often more primal.

I have also discovered within each group some recognizable behavioral patterns will emerge when each is presented with an adverse situation. In other words, when it hits the fan, most people will fling it back at the fan. Satan loves this because the bad behavior will spread over a greater distance, which will cause others to reciprocate. But, those within the Body of Christ will not allow the matter to escalate; they will assume the role of Peacemaker. And, if it does escalate, they will get a metaphorical mop and attempt to clean up the mess by turning the other cheek. "Therefore all things whatsoever ye would that men should do to you, do ye even so to them: for this is the law and the prophets. 13 Enter ye in at the strait gate: for wide is the gate, and broad is the way, that leadeth to destruction, and many there be which go in thereat:" (Matthew 7:12-13).

I often share with people a belief I live by - A godly life is not predicated on how people treat you; it is predicated on how you treat people. And unfortunately, I have discovered it mostly falls upon deaf ears. It is truly disheartening when people are no longer concerned about the Golden Rule. Most people do not realize that life consists of a series of tests. The early Saints call them Trails and Tribulations. "My brethren, count it all joy when ye fall into divers temptations; 3 Knowing this, that the trying of your faith worketh patience." (James 1:2-3). What upsets me is most people continue to fail life's tests. This is troubling when you consider God made all our tests - open Book. We live in a world in which everyone is treating people the way people are treating them, which is without love. "Beloved, let us love one another: for love is of God, and every one that loveth is born of God, and knoweth God. 8 He that loveth not knoweth not God; for God is love." (1 John 4:7-8). I reiterate my earlier point. If Jesus is in the midst of a situation, no matter what the situation may be, his presence will immensely improve the circumstances within that situation. For example, if a couple allows Jesus to come into their marriage, the love and trust that would develop in that relationship would truly astound them and their friends.

"And Adam said, This is now bone of my bones, and flesh of my flesh: she shall be called Woman, because she was taken out of Man. 24 Therefore shall a man leave his father and his mother, and shall cleave unto his wife: and they shall be one flesh." (Genesis 2:23-24). When you purchase a house, if you allow Jesus to participate, your newly purchased house will become a loving and happy home. "Behold, I stand at the door, and knock: if any man hear my voice, and open the door, I will come in to him, and will sup with him, and he with me." (Revelation 3:20). Also, one of the residual side effects of having Jesus in your life and in your home is that he makes you a better person and a better neighbor. "And he answering said, Thou shalt love the Lord thy God with all thy heart, and with all thy soul, and with all thy strength, and with all thy mind; and thy neighbour as thyself." (Luke 10:27). If people in business allow Jesus to be the guiding principle in their decision process, the Bible states they and their business would flourish. "A false balance is abomination to the Lord: but a just weight is his delight. 3 The integrity of the upright shall guide them: but the perverseness of transgressors shall destroy them. 4 Riches profit not in the day of wrath: but righteousness delivereth from death." (Proverbs 11:1,3-4). If parents place their children on the path to follow Jesus Christ, they will watch them grow into righteous Adults. "Train up a child in the way he should go: and when he is old, he will not depart from it." (Proverbs 22:6).

Naturally naysayers will try to dispute these claims of righteousness through Jesus. But the one thing they surely cannot dispute is the rampant rise of sinful behavior and the moral decay within our society. The evidence of this is all over creation (e.g., mass shootings, incivility, racial hatred, and social injustice.) With this understanding, let’s apply my Jesus method again, but now let's reverse it. In other words, let's remove Jesus from the equation. For example, we have an extremely high divorce rate here in our country. The lawyers, therapists, sociologists, and marriage counselors who work with these divorcing couples will tell you the reasons behind such high rates are too numerous to count. I, too, have interacted with couples who are going through a divorce, and after much observation. I can give you two words that explain the high divorce rate in America. Those two words are, no Jesus. In many cases, the disgruntled couple seeking to end their marriage began that marriage standing before God, a minister, friends, and family. However, at some point in their marriage, the couple eventually stopped standing before God and yielding to the wisdom of His Word. Those of us in ministry know that it is a recipe for disaster when God is left out of the equation, especially in a marriage. Let me take it a step further. What is the common denominator between a rapist, a wife beater, a fornicator, a liar, a thief, and a murderer - no Jesus. Here is a biblical example of what Jesus brings to the table. "Therefore if any man be in Christ, he is a new creature: old things are passed away; behold, all things are become new." (2 Corinthians 5:17). Let's examine this scripture more closely, starting with the opening statement - if any man be in Christ. The apostle Paul has made a clear and convincing declaration here. It means a person has had the wherewithal to seek out and surrender his life to Christ. This is surely a miracle because two-thirds of the global population currently have not discovered our Lord and Savior. "Because strait is the gate, and narrow is the way, which leadeth unto life, and few there be that find it." (Matthew 7:14).

There are many who feel that their previous actions in life would hinder or deny them a second chance to access anything considered good and decent. But, because of the sacrifice of Jesus Christ, we are not denied entry into the Kingdom of God, no matter what we may have done. "I am the door: by me if any man enter in, he shall be saved, and shall go in and out, and find pasture." (John 10:9). Second Corinthians chapter 5 verse 17 helps the Believer recognize the awesome gift of God's grace. Especially when you consider what some of us have done. Some have killed, some have stolen, and others have abandoned their families, etc. None of that sinful behavior disqualifies a person from taking refuge in Christ Jesus. It is hard to fathom that some within humanity could rise to an acceptable standard for God. Just consider how Mankind has said many within their ranks are unfit or undeserving of basic kindness or equality. "And it came to pass, that, as Jesus sat at meat in his house, many publicans and sinners sat also together with Jesus and his disciples: for there were many, and they followed him. 16 And when the scribes and Pharisees saw him eat with publicans and sinners, they said unto his disciples, How is it that he eateth and drinketh with publicans and sinners? 17 When Jesus heard it, he saith unto them, They that are whole have no need of the physician, but they that are sick: I came not to call the righteous, but sinners to repentance." (Mark 2:15-17). Unfortunately, life will not allow you access to many things you may believe you have a right to. But what a joy it is to know; no matter what your sins and shortcomings are, God loves you and will welcome you with open arms. “For I will be merciful to their unrighteousness, and their sins and their iniquities will I remember no more.” (Hebrews 8:12).

What is it like to be a new creature? We all have heard someone say to a person that has lost weight, "I barely recognize you, or you look great, or what's your secret?". These statements could be true, and the person’s outward appearance may have undergone drastic changes due to weight loss. But weight loss, no matter how extreme, does not truly change what a person looks like on the inside. If he was a cheapskate when he was overweight, odds are, he is still cheap. The only difference is that now he's a cheapskate with a plausible excuse - it can be difficult retrieving your wallet in skinny jeans. The distinction of being a new creature in Christ is accountable for the characteristics and properties of God changing the inward man. Which, in turn, causes a noticeable change of behavior in the outward man. "But the Lord said unto Samuel, Look not on his countenance, or on the height of his stature; because I have refused him: for the Lord seeth not as man seeth; for man looketh on the outward appearance, but the Lord looketh on the heart." (1 Samuel 16:7).

Herein lies the problem, as a new creature, we must leave the past in the past. Remember the example in Chapter 4, The Devil You Know. The Children of Israel refused to possess their Promised Land because mentally, they were bound to their past. In today's society, sinner and saint alike, many marriages are destroyed because a spouse would not free themselves from the damages of a past relationship. It is almost comical when you think about it.

Here is an example. Bob, a fellow Christian, ruined his marriage with his faithful, loving wife, Susan, a godly woman because he did not trust her. Bob did not trust Susan because he was in a toxic relationship with an ungodly woman named Tracy, who cheated on him five years earlier. When you realize this type of mistrust is common in today's marriages, you soon discover it is no longer a laughing matter. Here's another familiar example of not leaving the past in the past. Have you ever heard someone say, "I will forgive, but I won't forget"? Let's use our friend Bob again for this story. Now that Bob is newly divorced from Susan, he has fallen on hard times. So, he borrows $100 from Mark, a co-worker and a member of his church. Bob promised Mark that he would pay him back on their next payday. I am sure you know what happened, a week turned into months, and Bob never paid Mark back the money he borrowed. Since Mark was a Christian, he forgave Bob but said he would never forget what Bod did. As Children of God, we really must help others understand that true forgiveness is to cease to remember how someone offended you. "This is the covenant that I will make with them after those days, saith the Lord, I will put my laws into their hearts, and in their minds will I write them; 17 And their sins and iniquities will I remember no more." (Hebrews 10:16-17). God made with us His chosen children a new and more excellent Covenant through His Son, Jesus Christ. Not only will God forgive His Children of their sins, He will also forget their sins completely. What is the lesson learned from this scripture? In short, if Bob was to ask Mark to loan him another $100, as a true Christian, Mark should loan him the money.

Because according to God, the previous unpaid debt should not be a factor in Mark's decision since true forgiveness is to forget. "Then came Peter to him, and said, Lord, how oft shall my brother sin against me, and I forgive him? till seven times? 22 Jesus saith unto him, I say not unto thee, Until seven times: but, Until seventy times seven." (Matthew 18:21-22).

When we consider the many sins we have committed against God and how God has forgiven and forgotten them all, how could we not forgive our brothers and sisters of their trivial offenses? "And unto him that smiteth thee on the one cheek offer also the other; and him that taketh away thy cloak forbid not to take thy coat also. 30 Give to every man that asketh of thee; and of him that taketh away thy goods ask them not again. 31 And as ye would that men should do to you, do ye also to them likewise. 32 For if ye love them which love you, what thank have ye? for sinners also love those that love them. 33 And if ye do good to them which do good to you, what thank have ye? for sinners also do even the same. 34 And if ye lend to them of whom ye hope to receive, what thank have ye? for sinners also lend to sinners, to receive as much again. 35 But love ye your enemies, and do good, and lend, hoping for nothing again; and your reward shall be great, and ye shall be the children of the Highest: for he is kind unto the unthankful and to the evil. 36 Be ye therefore merciful, as your Father also is merciful. 37 Judge not, and ye shall not be judged: condemn not, and ye shall not be condemned: forgive, and ye shall be forgiven: 38 Give, and it shall be given unto you; good measure, pressed down, and shaken together, and running over, shall men give into your bosom. For with the same measure that ye mete withal it shall be measured to you again." (Luke 6:29-38). Luke is describing the behavior of the New Creature. The circumstances in life remain the same, but how we respond to those circumstances has changed. Luke shows Believers they can move confidently in Christ Jesus as a New Creature, fully knowing those things which were lost are considered gain in the Kingdom of God. What a wonderful mindset.

The past or those things of Adam are dead and buried, and our future is filled with the newness of Christ Jesus. And above all, being a new creature in Christ is to change old behavior and willingly accept the teachings of Jesus. Remember, you are as a little child, and a child learns from his Father. When the old man was offended, he would fight, but the new man prays. The old creature was selfish; the new creature is generous.

This brings me to my final point; this statement may face conflict and controversy. Because some of the things I am about to share with you may not have been shared before within your Faith-based community. As you have seen, we inherited a lot from Adam, and none of it was good. "Wherefore, as by one man sin entered into the world, and death by sin; and so death passed upon all men, for that all have sinned:" (Romans 5:12). I know I have quoted this verse before in a previous Chapter, but it bears repeating and with greater detail. Romans chapter 5, verse 12 states that sin and death entered the world because of Adam's disobedience. And because Adam disobeyed his God, we, the human offspring of Adam, are all born sinners, and we will all die. Absent supernatural intervention, this is our fate; we have no choice in the matter. That's right, No Choice or No Free Will. We do not choose to be a Sinner or a Saint. From the onset, we are all sinners on our way to Hell. But, glory is to God; in the fullness of time, which was about two thousand years ago, He designed a way out for some of the Sin-Cursed Children of Adam. "But when the fulness of the time was come, God sent forth his Son, made of a woman, made under the law, 5 To redeem them that were under the law, that we might receive the adoption of sons." (Galatians 4:4-5). Through Jesus Christ, we can become Sinners Saved by Grace, and thus a Sinner no more. Do not confuse the gift of Jesus and our ability to accept Christ as Free Will. Our choice is not identical to the Free Will God gave Adam and Eve; they are not one and the same. As stated earlier, Christ was born two thousand years ago, eventually allowing Mankind a choice.

That choice is not to be confused with the Free Will granted Adam at Creation. Consider this; if you believe the choice you were given through Jesus is Free Will, then you have proven my point. It cannot be the same Free Will God gave Adam. Because, the semblance of Free Will that you are basing your premise upon only arrived after Christ was Crucified at Calvary. To intertwine Free Will with the gift of Jesus, denies Free Will to the millions upon millions that lived and died in their sins before Christ the Savior was ever born. In your premise, where was their choice or their Free Will? The lofty dream of today's Free Will, is only a concoction by some lost to the whims of Gentile men. I might also add that your premise is further flawed because the choice of Christ Jesus was originally only intended for the Children of Israel. Once again, denying the rest of Humanity an opportunity to choose. "And, behold, a woman of Canaan came out of the same coasts, and cried unto him, saying, Have mercy on me, O Lord, thou son of David; my daughter is grievously vexed with a devil. 24 But he answered and said, I am not sent but unto the lost sheep of the house of Israel." (Matthew 15:22,24).

In Man's current sin state, what he perceives as Free Will is just the freedom Satan gives him to choose what type of sinner he wants to be. A bad sinner, an evil sinner, or a really, really bad sinner, but a sinner nonetheless. Hear me and hear me well, Man surrendered Free Will when he sinned in the Garden of Eden. Free Will was a Characteristic of the Likeness of God from which Adam was Created thereof and subsequently lost. Free Will does not exist in this earthly realm outside of God. Those who have it received it after and not before we chose Jesus, the Son of God. "And ye shall know the truth, and the truth shall make you free. 33 They answered him, We be Abraham's seed, and were never in bondage to any man: how sayest thou, Ye shall be made free? 34 Jesus answered them, Verily, verily, I say unto you, Whosoever committeth sin is the servant of sin. 35 And the servant abideth not in the house for ever: but the Son abideth ever.

36 If the Son therefore shall make you free, ye shall be free indeed." (John 8:32-36). Adam and Eve were the only Humans ever to have Free Will outside of the Body of Jesus the Messiah. Unlike the Angels who did not have Free Will because they were created for a particular service or purpose; (e.g., messenger, guardian, praise.) "And the angel answering said unto him, I am Gabriel, that stand in the presence of God; and am sent to speak unto thee, and to shew thee these glad tidings." (Luke 1:19). "Behold, I send an Angel before thee, to keep thee in the way, and to bring thee into the place which I have prepared." (Exodus 23:20). "Praise ye him, all his angels: praise ye him, all his hosts." (Psalm 148:2).

God gifted Adam and Eve with Free Will for the sole purpose of love. They could choose Freely what type of loving relationship they wanted with the God of Creation. It would be of their own accord and not by God's design. Adam's Free Will never consisted of a choice between God and Satan. Nothing in all of Creation could stand equal to God, so a choice between equal parts could not be made. "To whom then will ye liken me, or shall I be equal? saith the Holy One." (Isaiah 40:25). Please, I encourage you to reread the Creation story, but this time, desire to read it in the Spirit. With God's gift of the Holy Spirit, you will understand God did not give Adam Free Will or a Choice to eat from The Tree of Knowledge. God told Adam he could eat freely of every tree but not of that Tree. "And the Lord God commanded the man, saying, Of every tree of the garden thou mayest freely eat: 17 But of the tree of the knowledge of good and evil, thou shalt not eat of it: for in the day that thou eatest thereof thou shalt surely die." (Genesis 2:16-17). Once again, God created Adam and Eve with Free Will, so they could develop Freely the type of loving relationship they would have with God.

"I love the Lord, because he hath heard my voice and my supplications. 2 Because he hath inclined his ear unto me, therefore will I call upon him as long as I live." (Psalm 116:1-2).

Chapter Nine

THE KINGDOM OF HEAVEN

"From that time Jesus began to preach, and to say, Repent: for the kingdom of heaven is at hand." (Matthew 4:17).

The term Kingdom of Heaven has perplexed many Theologians for centuries. What is it? When is it? Where is it? How does it work? How do you get in, and who is allowed in? The Bible contains scriptures indicating the Disciples also had concerns about the Kingdom of Heaven. "At the same time came the disciples unto Jesus, saying, Who is the greatest in the kingdom of heaven? 2 And Jesus called a little child unto him, and set him in the midst of them, 3 And said, Verily I say unto you, Except ye be converted, and become as little children, ye shall not enter into the kingdom of heaven. 4 Whosoever therefore shall humble himself as this little child, the same is greatest in the kingdom of heaven." (Matthew 18:1-4). In the King James Bible, the term Kingdom of Heaven only appears in the Gospel of St Matthew. In the remaining Gospels, Jesus uses another term - the Kingdom of God. Notice how Jesus states the little child scripture in the books of Mark and Luke differently than how he stated it in the book of Matthew. "Verily I say unto you, Whosoever shall not receive the kingdom of God as a little child, he shall not enter therein." (Mark 10:15). "Verily I say unto you, Whosoever shall not receive the kingdom of God as a little child shall in no wise enter therein." (Luke 18:17). The terms the Kingdom of Heaven and the Kingdom of God are not interchangeable. But there is an exception.

Allow me to explain. In the little child representations, yes, they are interchangeable. However, in other scriptures, the terms are not interchangeable because the Kingdom of Heaven and the Kingdom of God can represent two separate places. For instance, notice how Jesus uses the same phrase in the following scripture when he speaks of the Kingdom where his Father God resides in the Heavenly realm. "There shall be weeping and gnashing of teeth, when ye shall see Abraham, and Isaac, and Jacob, and all the prophets, in the kingdom of God, and you yourselves thrust out." (Luke 13:28). As it related to Jesus and only Jesus, the only difference between the Kingdom of Heaven and the Kingdom of God was the location.

Here's an interesting fact, God allowed Jacob to see how the two Kingdoms interacted. A sort of upstairs and downstairs view. "And Jacob went out from Beersheba, and went toward Haran. 11 And he lighted upon a certain place, and tarried there all night, because the sun was set; and he took of the stones of that place, and put them for his pillows, and lay down in that place to sleep. 12 And he dreamed, and behold a ladder set up on the earth, and the top of it reached to heaven: and behold the angels of God ascending and descending on it." (Genesis 28:10-12). Jesus operated in this earthly realm as he did in the heavenly realm. He knew the physical world was framed on the greater and unseen spiritual world. This meant the physical principles of our World did not apply to Jesus because of who he was and what he knew. "In the beginning was the Word, and the Word was with God, and the Word was God. 2 The same was in the beginning with God. 3 All things were made by him; and without him was not any thing made that was made." (John 1:1-3). As was forementioned, as it relates to Jesus and only Jesus Christ, the only difference between the Kingdom of Heaven and the Kingdom of God was the location. And, both also represent Jesus' original home. Observe his action as it relates to the Scientific Laws of our World. "And when he had spoken these things, while they beheld, he was taken up; and a cloud received him out of their sight." (Acts 1:9). As you can see, the Law of Gravity did not affect Jesus. No earthly Law could or would restrain the power and purpose of Jesus. He demonstrated this very fact with his first known miracle. "And the third day there was a marriage in Cana of Galilee; and the mother of Jesus was there: 2 And both Jesus was called, and his disciples, to the marriage. 3 And when they wanted wine, the mother of Jesus saith unto him, They have no wine. 4 Jesus saith unto her, Woman, what have I to do with thee? mine hour is not yet come. 5 His mother saith unto the servants, Whatsoever he saith unto you, do it. 6 And there were set there six waterpots of stone, after the manner of the purifying of the Jews, containing two or three firkins apiece. 7 Jesus saith unto them, Fill the waterpots with water. And they filled them up to the brim. 8 And he saith unto them, Draw out now, and bear unto the governor of the feast. And they bare it. 9 When the ruler of the feast had tasted the water that was made wine, and knew not whence it was: (but the servants which drew the water knew;) the governor of the feast called the bridegroom, 10 And saith unto him, Every man at the beginning doth set forth good wine; and when men have well drunk, then that which is worse: but thou hast kept the good wine until now. 11 This beginning of miracles did Jesus in Cana of Galilee, and manifested forth his glory; and his disciples believed on him." (John 2:1-11).

I trust that now you also see how perplexing the term the Kingdom of Heaven is, and with this understanding, follow my attempt at clarifying this matter with you. As I clarify elements of the Kingdom of Heaven, I will provide biblical and earthly examples to prove my point. What is the Kingdom of Heaven? The Kingdom of Heaven is the earthly twin of the Kingdom of God. The Kingdom of God is the traditional Heaven we know all too well, wherein God resides with the Angels and our loved ones who have died in Christ. In the Kingdom of God, His Will and Word are absolute. Through His Son Jesus of Nazareth, God has duplicated the Kingdom of God here on Earth in the guise of the Kingdom of Heaven.

Here's the Biblical example I mentioned earlier wherein you will see the duplication aspect I spoke of manifested in verse 2. "And it came to pass, that, as he was praying in a certain place, when he ceased, one of his disciples said unto him, Lord, teach us to pray, as John also taught his disciples. 2 And he said unto them, When ye pray, say, Our Father which art in heaven, Hallowed be thy name. Thy kingdom come. Thy will be done, as in heaven, so in earth." (Luke 11:1-2).

The following will be an earthly example of the Kingdom of Heaven. We are all familiar with the Governmental concept of an Embassy. It is the physical representation of a Sovereign Nation on foreign soil, and the people that work within that Embassy have what is called Diplomatic Immunity. This means the personnel stationed at that Embassy are not bound by the rules, regulations, and laws of the host Country in which their Embassy is located. For instance, the person in charge of the Saudi Embassy here in the United States could be a Saudi Prince. As a Diplomatic Representative or Ambassador for his Country, he and the Embassy staff are governed by the laws of Saudi Arabia, which is Sharia Law, not the Constitution of the United States. Here is my point, the Saudi Prince is allowed to practice Polygamy here in America. He is allowed to do so because it is legal in Saudi Arabia. So, he suffers no legal consequence here in America, where Polygamy is illegal. Furthermore, any U.S. citizens entering the Saudi Embassy must abide by the rules, regulations, and laws of Saudi Arabia. My point is; the Kingdom of Heaven can be viewed in this manner. Although located here on Earth, it is ruled and governed by God and His Laws. As you may see, this Embassy example can be an excellent model to show us, the Children of God, what true Kingdom living is and its tremendous potential. "But ye are a chosen generation, a royal priesthood, an holy nation, a peculiar people; that ye should shew forth the praise of him who hath called you out of darkness into his marvelous light;" (1 Peter 2:9).

The Children of God, have had all of the Powers of God's Heavenly Authority bestows upon them. "For the kingdom of God is not in word, but in power." (1 Corinthians 4:20).
If we could ever fully understand the privileges gifted to us through Christ Jesus and the Kingdom of Heaven, oh, the miracles we could perform. "Verily, verily, I say unto you, He that believeth on me, the works that I do shall he do also; and greater works than these shall he do; because I go unto my Father." (John 14:12). Please do your best to try and comprehend this. The Kingdom of Heaven is a Sovereign Holy Nation. As an Ambassador of the Kingdom of Heaven Believers have Spiritual Diplomatic Immunity. In a nutshell, this means Scientific Laws or Man-made Laws do not rule over Believers. The Apostles understood this very fact. Let us observe Peter and Paul as examples. They ignored the laws of Men. "Then came one and told them, saying, Behold, the men whom ye put in prison are standing in the temple, and teaching the people. 26 Then went the captain with the officers, and brought them without violence: for they feared the people, lest they should have been stoned. 27 And when they had brought them, they set them before the council: and the high priest asked them, 28 Saying, Did not we straitly command you that ye should not teach in this name? and, behold, ye have filled Jerusalem with your doctrine, and intend to bring this man's blood upon us. 29 Then Peter and the other apostles answered and said, We ought to obey God rather than men." (Acts 5:25-29). Also, the laws of Science did not constrain them. "And there sat in a window a certain young man named Eutychus, being fallen into a deep sleep: and as Paul was long preaching, he sunk down with sleep, and fell down from the third loft, and was taken up dead. 10 And Paul went down, and fell on him, and embracing him said, Trouble not yourselves; for his life is in him." (Acts 20:9-10).

Here is my testimony about Kingdom Living. At the beginning of the book, I asked you for prayer as a hedge of protection for my family and myself as I wrote the book.

However, when I typed my request to you, I understood that you had not yet received or read the book. As a resident within the Kingdom of Heaven, I and others live by faith. We know faith is the foundation and gravity upon which the Kingdom of Heaven is built. "Now faith is the substance of things hoped for, the evidence of things not seen." (Hebrews 11:1). Let me further explain. As you have learned, within the Kingdom of Heaven, God is our King. It is governed by the Supernatural Principles of His powers and His authority, not by Man's natural abilities. So, when I requested prayer as an inhabitant of God's Kingdom, God dispatched the response to a fellow dweller within the Kingdom of Heaven. And that person or persons, whoever they may have been, prayed for me, a stranger that they did not know. Have you ever prayed for someone who did not ask you directly for prayer? A stranger you saw in passing and felt led by the Spirit to speak a word to the Father on their behalf. That is a sign of Kingdom Living. Meaning, your wireless fidelity (Wi-Fi) is connected to the Kingdom of Heaven, and you constantly receive and send messages. With your new understanding of Kingdom Residency, I would like to thank those of you for your prayers of support. "Praying always with all prayer and supplication in the Spirit, and watching thereunto with all perseverance and supplication for all saints;" (Ephesians 6:18).

Here is an example of the metaphysical power of prayer. I once told a friend experiencing hardship that I would pray for God's protection over him. My friend jokingly replied, “God has been protecting me long before I ever knew you!”. I informed my friend that very protection came about because of my prayers. Naturally, he was dumbfounded, so I explained to him the true supernatural abilities of prayer. I told him that I have a relative that’s a Fireman and his mother often prays that God keep a hedge of protection around her son. Most believe, as my friend believed, that the mother’s prayer covers the son on the day that she prayed, as well as future days to come. You see, we perceive Time as linear, meaning it moves forward on a straight line.

Man perceives Time as Yesterday, Today, and Tomorrow. However, God is not bound by our concept of Time. To God, every day is Now. Today is now, yesterday is now, and tomorrow is now. This meant God heard the mother's prayer and protected her son from the fires he fought the day of the prayer. And fires he would face in the future, but the prayer also covered the son when he fought his first fire at the beginning of his career. According to scripture, the mother's prayer traveled throughout time, and God protected her son long before he became a Fireman and long before she became a mother. “According as he hath chosen us in him before the foundation of the world, that we should be holy and without blame before him in love:” (Ephesian 1:4). Here's a Biblical example of God, Man, and a Timeline. "Now Jericho was straitly shut up because of the children of Israel: none went out, and none came in. 2 And the Lord said unto Joshua, See, I have given into thine hand Jericho, and the king thereof, and the mighty men of valour. 3 And ye shall compass the city, all ye men of war, and go round about the city once. Thus shalt thou do six days. 4 And seven priest shall bear before the ark seven trumpets of rams' horns: and the seventh day ye shall compass the city seven times, and the priests shall blow with the trumpets. 5 And it shall come to pass, that when they make a long blast with the ram's horn, and when ye hear the sound of the trumpet, all the people shall shout with a great shout; and the wall of the city shall fall down flat, and the people shall ascend up every man straight before him." (Joshua 6:1-5). As it relates to God, the battle was over, and Jericho had fallen into the hands of Joshua and the Children of Israel. As it relates to Joshua, he has yet to see a victory against the city of Jericho because he’s still located outside of the city. The walls were still intact and the king was safe inside. In Joshua’s timeline, the victory was seven days away.

Now that we know how the Kingdom of Heaven operates and that it is a shared experience. From this point, let us ask some deeper, more personal, or specific questions. One such question some may ask is whether the Kingdom of Heaven is still at hand or has it come, and if not, when will it come? By my examples and after spiritually discerning the times, the answer is "yes." Rejoice the Kingdom of Heaven has arrived. And glory is to God; it came by way of the Cross at Calvary. "And I, if I be lifted up from the earth, will draw all men unto me." (John 12:32). And, on the Day of Pentecost, the Kingdom of Heaven became fully recognizable, operational, and received some of its first residents. "And when the day of Pentecost was fully come, they were all with one accord in one place. 2 And suddenly there came a sound from heaven as of a rushing mighty wind, and it filled all the house where they were sitting. 3 And there appeared unto them cloven tongues like as of fire, and it sat upon each of them. 4 And they were all filled with the Holy Ghost, and began to speak with other tongues, as the spirit gave them utterance." (Acts 2:1-4). Another question some may ask about the Kingdom of Heaven is where is it located? On the Day of Pentecost, the Kingdom of Heaven was located in Jerusalem. But according to Jesus, the location of the Kingdom of Heaven varies, ranging from today being in America and tomorrow being in Africa. It is not located in just one place, and it is expanding. "Not every one that saith unto me, Lord, Lord, shall enter into the kingdom of heaven; but he that doeth the will of my Father which is in heaven." (Matthew 7:21). Jesus told his followers that the Kingdom of Heaven is located anywhere Men are doing the Will of his Father, wherever that may be. By doing God's Will, one gains entrance into the Kingdom of Heaven, which brings about that growth I mention earlier. "Again, the kingdom of heaven is like unto a net, that was cast into the sea, and gathered of every kind: 48 Which, when it was full, they drew to shore, and sat down, and gathered the good into vessels, but cast the bad away." (Matthew 13:47-48).

Please highlight Matthew chapter 7, verse 21; we will look at it in greater detail in the next chapter, The End Is Near.

Some may ask a more personal question about how one can access the Kingdom of Heaven. Does there exist other ways in which an individual can become a resident of the Kingdom of Heaven? A shortcut or a test? "Blessed are the poor in spirit: for theirs is the kingdom of heaven. 10 Blessed are they which are persecuted for righteousness' sake: for theirs is the kingdom of heaven." (Matthew 5:3,10). The Apostle Peter played a major role in granting access into the Kingdom of Heaven. "And I say also unto thee, That thou art Peter, and upon this rock I will build my church; and the gates of hell shall not prevail against it. 19 And I will give unto thee the keys of the kingdom of heaven: and whatsoever thou shalt bind on earth shall be bound in heaven: and whatsoever thou shalt loose on earth shall be loosed in heaven." (Matthew 16:18-19). It was not by chance that Peter was the Disciple who preached on the Day of Pentecost. He was the chosen Shepard opening the gate for the Master's new flock. "But Peter, standing up with the eleven, lifted up his voice, and said unto them, Ye men of Judaea, and all ye that dwell at Jerusalem, be this known unto you, and hearken to my words: 22 Ye men of Israel, hear these words; Jesus of Nazareth, a man approved of God among you by miracles and wonders and signs, which God did by him in the midst of you, as ye yourselves also know: 37 Now when they heard this, they were pricked in their heart, and said unto Peter and to the rest of the apostles, Men and brethren, what shall we do? 38 Then Peter said unto them, Repent, and be baptized every one of you in the name of Jesus Christ for the remission of sins, and ye shall receive the gift of the Holy Ghost. 41 Then they that gladly received his word were baptized: and the same day there were added unto them about three thousand souls." (Acts 2:14,22,37-38,41).

Here's one difference between the two Kingdoms. Jesus never said being Good will allow a person entrance into God's Kingdom. Nevertheless, most believe they are going to Heaven because they are Good.

I hear this repeatedly from people who have not been Born Again. And, what is truly horrifying is everyone believes that they are surely Good. The thief believes he's good. The adulterer believes he's good. Even the gangster believes he's good because he gives away Turkeys at Thanksgiving. I once had a co-worker that everyone considered, a Jerk. People would leave when this guy entered the room because no one wanted to be around him. One day this man asked me why do people leave when he comes into a room. I told him it was because people felt he was awful. Much to my surprise, this man was utterly shocked by my response. He was not aware of the others' sentiment toward him. He thought of himself as a Good person. The simple reason that Jesus omitted being Good as a way to gain entrance into the Kingdom of God is that none of us are good. However, the reasons people say none are Good vary from the physical to the spiritual. For instance, many say we are not Good because we are made from the Dust of the Ground. This means if cleanliness is next to Godliness, then we are actually Dirty without spiritual intervention. However, many still believe they are good enough to gain entrance into Heaven. Unfortunately, good people will find themselves in the same place reserved for bad people, Hell. To avoid this fiery fate, we must obey God's Word and follow Jesus. "And, behold, one came and said unto him, Good Master, what good thing shall I do, that I may have eternal life? 17 And he said unto him, Why callest thou me good? there is none good but one, that is, God: but if thou wilt enter into life, keep the commandments. 18 He saith unto him, Which? Jesus said, Thou shalt do no murder, Thou shalt not commit adultery, Thou shalt not steal, Thou shalt not bear false witness, 19 Honour thy father and thy mother: and, Thou shalt love thy neighbour as thyself. 20 The young man saith unto him, All these things have I kept from my youth up: what lack I yet? 21 Jesus said unto him, if thou wilt be perfect, go and sell that thou hast, and give to the poor, and thou shalt have treasure in heaven: and come and follow me." (Matthew 19:16-21).

There is only one remaining question left to share and discuss. Although, I have already provided some examples beforehand. I will now humbly explain how the Kingdom of Heaven works. For believers, explaining this Kingdom can be a simple and complex proposition all in one. Simple in that the Kingdom of Heaven operates diametrically differently than this world or the Kingdom of Men. Picture it this way. If it is acceptable behavior in this world, odds are it's not acceptable in the Kingdom of Heaven. If Men consider it important here, trust me, it's not important in the Kingdom of Heaven. If it is impossible in this world, it is entirely possible in the Kingdom of Heaven. If it is hated in this world, more than likely, it is loved in the Kingdom of Heaven. One way you can tell how close you are to God, is by measuring how far you are from Man. If men speak highly of you, people love you, you're the life of the party, and everyone enjoys having you around. Let me warn you. If you like those accolades, and you travel this road called life trying to satisfy Man, chances are great that you are being led away from God. "If the world hate you, ye know that it hated me before it hated you. 19 If ye were of the world, the world would love his own: but because ye are not of the world, but I have chosen you out of the world, therefore the world hateth you." (John 15:18-19).

This hate is as old as time itself. At this point, it is easy to understand how two opposing forces, or two Kingdoms, can result in a putrid, sinister, and revolting form of hatred emanating from the world and designed to devour the Soul. I want to discuss one example of this hatred and how it came to be within the Faith. I will discuss through scripture why this hatred should be a non-issue within the Kingdom of Heaven. But, unfortunately, it has become a central component. This hate should only be an issue in the Kingdom of Men, where there is an absence of Spiritual Wisdom. Within the discriminatory Kingdom of Men, Women are devalued and face Sexism on a daily basis. Numerous people believe Women are not suited for certain positions in life: such as President, CEO, and sadly, Pastor.

Their sentiments are primarily based on the belief that women are not as strong as men and they are the weaker Vessel. I would like to point out that the Bible never said or inferred Eve was the weaker Vessel before Original Sin. God assigned **Them**, man and woman, to have dominion over all the Earth. Not Adam alone, nor Eve, but both as **Equals**. "And God said, Let us make man in our image, after our likeness: and let them have dominion over the fish of the sea, and over the fowl of the air, and over the cattle, and over all the earth, and over every creeping thing that creepeth upon the earth." (Genesis 1:26). Also, according to the Bible, as it relates to God, He viewed both the man and the woman as **Adam**. "This is the book of generations of Adam. In the day that God created man, in the likeness of God made he him; 2 Male and female created he them; and blessed them, and called their name Adam, in the day when they were created. (Genesis 5:1-2). Here begets an interesting point. The woman was not called Eve until after they had Sinned. "And Adam called his wife's name Eve; because she was the mother of all living." (Genesis 3:20). This next scripture reveals how Eve was downgraded, and Adam was elevated to rule over her as a direct punishment for her Sins. "Unto the woman he said, I will greatly multiply thy sorrow and thy conception; in sorrow thou shalt bring forth children; and thy desire shall be to thy husband, and he shall rule over thee." (Genesis 3:16).

Now here's where it becomes problematic. Consider, if you will, how would you explain a concept like love or hate to an Alien Race with no knowledge of Human Emotions. And how can you describe a woman that is completely equal to a man in every aspect of her being? When Humanity has never seen such a Creature. Well, here goes nothing. It would be best if you relied on the Holy Spirit to guide you to grasp what I will write next. Also, remember you relied on the Spirit when you believed that Moses parted the Red Sea. You relied on the Spirit when you understood the story of the three Hebrew boys and the Fiery Furnace.

And you definitely relied on the Holy Spirit when you believed a Virgin gave birth to a Son. All these examples are true and point to the awesome Power of God. But only if you lean not unto your own understanding.

So why is a woman being completely equal to a man such a touchy subject within Christianity? If you read Genesis chapter 3, verse 16 in the Spirit, you will see part of Eve's punishment did and would affect her Physical Body. And, it is highly possible this physical transformation rendered her weaker than her male counterpart. Also, it seems her punishment may have had less to do with her Gender and more to do with the order in which God passed out His lasting judgment. If you take a closer look at the order and administering of the punishment, you will find that it moved from the greater offender to the least of the offenders.

First, we see God starts with the Architect of the sinful ordeal. God Curses the demonic Serpent to a horrible existence. The second offender to whom God deals judgment to is Eve. We soon will discover that her punishment would affect her Mental and her Physical well-being. The final offender God administers punishment to is Adam. After we read the scriptures concerning his punishment, one thing becomes quite clear and plain. Adam's punishment is not as severe as the other two offenders. Not to make light of it, but it was primarily hard labor. Many in the Kingdom of Man would say Eve got what she deserved. Even today, some hate Eve, the Woman for her transgressions. But, we the Children of God residing in the Kingdom of Heaven, fully understand that Jesus Christ is our Redeemer. "And they sung a new song, saying, Thou art worthy to take the book, and to open the seals thereof: for thou wast slain, and hast redeemed us to God by thy blood out of every kindred, and tongue, and people, and nation;" (Revelation 5:9). The Bible has shown us, Mankind relies on distinctions between groups to give some basis for understanding each group, God does not. "For as many of you as have been baptized into Christ have put on Christ.

28 There is neither Jew nor Greek, there is neither bond nor free, there is neither male nor female: for ye are all one in Christ Jesus." (Galatians 3:27-28). The definition of Redeemed is to gain or regain possession of (something). So, through Christ Jesus, Man was Redeemed or Restored back to his former sinless Glory and allowed entry into the presence of God. "And you, that were sometime alienated and enemies in your mind by wicked works, yet now hath he reconciled 22 In the body of his flesh through death, to present you holy and unblameable and unreproveable in his sight:" (Colossians 1:21-22). This means the Woman was also restored to her former sinless position, which was to reign with Man and not to be reigned over by Man. "And hast made us unto our God kings and priests: and we shall reign on the earth." (Revelation 5:10). Also, the first Gospel Message preached in the Kingdom of Heaven after Christ rose from the tomb was preached to and through a Woman, Mary Magdalene. "Jesus saith unto her, Woman, why weepiest thou? whom seekest thou? She, supposing him to be the gardener, saith unto him, Sir, if thou have borne him hence, tell me where thou hast laid him, and I will take him away. 16 Jesus saith unto her, Mary. She turned herself, and saith unto him, Rabboni; which is to say, Master. 17 Jesus saith unto her, Touch me not; for I am not yet ascend to my Father: but go to my brethren, and say unto them, I ascend unto my Father, and your Father; and to my God, and your God. 18 Mary Magdalene came and told the disciples that she had seen the Lord, and that he had spoken these things unto her." (John 20:15-18). Most in the Religious community will concede that Mary Magdalene did preach the first Gospel Message. But they will also say Preaching and Pastoring are not the same things, as stated by Paul in the Epistle of Timothy. "This is a true saying, if a man desire the office of a bishop, he desireth a good work. 2 A bishop then must be blameless, the husband of one wife, vigilant, sober, of good behaviour, given to hospitality, apt to teach;" (1 Timothy 3:1-2).

If this scripture is not read in the Spirit, it would appear as if Paul is saying only a Man can be a Bishop or Pastor. Based on the fact that only a Man can be a Husband. However, upon reading this scripture in the Spirit and with some historical reference, you will see that Paul was addressing a greater issue. One that could present itself as a problem for the new and emerging Faith - Polygamy.

Polygamous marriages were normal at this particular time in Israel and also in that part of the world. By the example of this scripture, Paul and the Christian Faith showed Israel and others that Polygamy was not what God wanted. First Timothy chapter 3 has nothing to do with the qualification of a woman in the office of a Bishop or Pastor. Only when you view it through the eyes of Sexism can you claim it prevents a woman from holding the office of a Bishop or Pastor. If you ignore the truth and use this scripture to support the tradition of Sexism, then you open the door for others to use scripture to support their tradition of Racism. Remember, just as you believe a woman cannot Pastor a congregation. Others believe a Black Man should not Pastor a white congregation. And, if you still believe a woman should not be a Pastor, answer me this? Who do you believe benefits the most from having fewer Pastors, God or Satan? “For whosoever shall call upon the name of the Lord shall be saved. 14 How then shall they call on him in whom they have not believe? and how shall they believe in him of whom they have not heard? and how shall they hear without a preacher?” (Romans 10:13-14).

These are the types of hatred that stand as examples of what makes the inner workings of the Kingdom of Heaven Complex. We seem torn between the two worlds, the Kingdom of Heaven and the Kingdom of Men. "And another also said, Lord, I will follow thee; but let me first go bid them farewell, which are at home at my house. 62 And Jesus said unto him, No man, having put his hand to the plough, and looking back, is fit for the kingdom of God." (Luke 9:61-62). A Believer being torn between the two worlds should be impossible, according to the

Apostle Paul. The Bible states that people living in the Kingdom of Heaven have died to this world of man. "Know ye not, that so many of us as were baptized into Jesus Christ were baptized into his death? 4 Therefore we are buried with him by baptism into death: that like as Christ was raised up from the dead by the glory of the Father, even so we also should walk in newness of life. 5 For if we have been planted together in the likeness of his death, we shall be also in the likeness of his resurrection: 6 Knowing this, that our old man is crucified with him, that the body of sin might be destroyed, that henceforth we should not serve sin. 7 For he that is dead is freed from sin." (Romans 6:3-7). This scripture states that we died with Christ so that the sin within us would be destroyed. Since this is true, did something follow us home from the Cemetery? Well, yes, earthly ills chase heavenly wills. The people within the Kingdom of Men constantly torment the residents of the Kingdom of Heaven. They continually chase and entice Believers with the desires of this world, wealth, status, and carnal pleasures. Which drives envy and hate. One word can describe their complete focus. That word is doubt, the antithesis of faith. Through faith, we should have a laser-like focus on our task, which is to lead every man, woman, and child from the Kingdom of Men into the Kingdom of Heaven. "Go ye therefore, and teach all nations, baptizing them in the name of the Father, and of the Son, and of the Holy Ghost:" (Matthew 28:19). As a new creature in Christ, we arise in the newness of life into our new world the Kingdom of Heaven. "Love not the world, neither the things that are in the world. If any man love the world, the love of the Father is not in him. 16 For all that is in the world, the lust of the flesh, and the lust of the eyes, and the pride of life, is not of the Father, but is of the world. 17 And the world passeth away, and the lust thereof: but he that doeth the will of God abideth for ever." (1 John 2:15-17).

Let us examine these scriptures, why does loving this world negate the love I have for God? Brace yourself. This may sting a bit but here goes nothing. Everything in this world is corrupt. Anything Man has ever touched or created has the Stain of Sin. Every known Institution on the planet is infected with sin. Every last government, corporation, business, banking, media, health care, education, and religion. Trust me; I hear people saying, "not Religion." Again, I hate to be the bearer of bad news, but yes, Religion is also stained by sin. And it requires no stretch of the imagination once you consider the numerous atrocities Humanity has committed in the name of Religion. And if you still have trouble believing my statement about Religion, we need to look no further than The Holy Land. There is no question that the land is Holy. However, the people that reside in and around the land behave somewhat differently. And that behavior has made God's Holy Land one of the most dangerous places on the Planet. And, it is not dangerous because the land is rich in Gold, Minerals, and Oil. No, it is dangerous because it is the focal point of the world's three major Religions - the most ominous trifecta feeding doubt and hate in the Kingdom of Man. Need I say more? Here's an example of how the stain of sin has infected an Industry.

Let's use the Health Care industry, with emphasis placed on Pharmaceuticals. Recently consumers have complained to the government that some of the new lifesaving drugs that have been produced cost more than what the average person makes in their lifetime. Many have been convinced that some Pharmaceutical Companies put profits before people. Sin is and can be a nuanced corruption filled with the pretense of good and hidden brutal objectives. Here's my experience with sin injecting hatred and doubt into one of our most popular institutions, the Hallowed Halls of Higher Education. As a young and naive college student, I remember enrolling in a class that I found somewhat troubling. The Professor taught that there was no such entity as God. He stated that God was a construct of Man's imagination created to control the uneducated masses.

This college Professor was the first Atheist I had ever met. I knew others who had not yet accepted Christ as their Lord and Savior, but I never met someone who did not believe in the existence of God. This was very shocking to me. Here was a person who had immense respect in the community but chose to use his platform - to shout from the rooftops and temple mounts, “there is no God” to young impressionable adults. Today, when my mind flashes to thoughts of his evil words. I continue to hope and pray that his teachings fell on deaf ears and God allowed him time to discover the truth. I hope God gives me the power of words to implode the evils spread through hatred and doubt. I pray that I am allowed to shine a bright righteous light upon misinformation dispersed by governments. Expose value propositions concocted by hatred and doubt sowed by businesses, corporations, and banking that put their bottom line ahead of people. Not by any means am I suggesting that the people that work in these industries are corrupt. On the contrary, most are pawns on a larger chessboard. We must bear witness to any entities that creates hate and doubt because Man created these Institutions. They created them in their own images, which means they were created flawed. "The Lord looked down from heaven upon the children of men, to see if there were any that did understand, and seek God. 3 They are all gone aside, they are all together become filthy: there is none that doeth good, no, not one." (Psalm 14:2-3).

I know this is hard to swallow, but please contemplate what I have said here. Examine or weigh these Institutions of Men by the Spirit of God. Once you have held them to the Light of the Truth, you will discover their foundations are not rooted in God, which means they are rooted in Satan by default. "They know not, neither will they understand; they walk on in darkness: all the foundations of the earth are out of course." (Psalm 82:5). I fondly remember my grandmother's testimony, having heard it many times during my childhood.

"On the solid rock of Jesus Christ, I stand; no storm can harm that precious land." "According to the grace of God which is given unto me, as a wise masterbuilder, I have laid the foundation, and another buildeth thereon. But let every man take heed how he buildeth thereupon. 11 For other foundation can no man lay than that is laid, which is Jesus Christ." (1 Corinthians 3:10-11).

Another dimension of the Kingdom of Man in complete opposition to the Kingdom of Heaven is the lust of the flesh. The lust of the flesh stands as one of the greatest threats to the Kingdom of Heaven in the world today. There was a wise Deacon at the Church where I was raised. And he would say, "if God doesn't punish America for its immorality, He is going to have to apologize to Sodom and Gomorrah." And what I find troubling about Deacon Brooks' statement is that he made it over 30 years ago. This was before Cell phones, and the Internet became intertwined in our daily lives. When Deacon Brooks made his statement, a twelve-year-old boy did not have easy access to Pornographic material in the palm of his hand. Neither did our daughters know the term Sexting. This was also before most men could carry hundreds of pornographic images in their photo apps. Today there are no bounds to the depths of our Sexual Immorality. Or in terms of the Kingdom of Man, the depths of our Sexual Freedom. Everything and anything truly is acceptable and even encouraged; nothing is off-limits within our society. For instance, many celebrate and impose illusions on the sensual body in their movies and music - regardless if the movie or the music is for kids or adults - and they receive more attention and accolades as they descend deeper into depravity. "Even as Sodom and Gomorrha, and the cities about them in like manner, giving themselves over to fornication, and going after strange flesh, are set forth for an example, suffering the vengeance of eternal fire." (Jude 1:7).

A few generations ago, the lust of the flesh was a young man's dilemma that would eventually run its course to the Marital bed. The prevailing thought used to be. Once our sons and daughters eventually married, fleshly lust would become a thing of the past and be replaced by Spiritual Maturity and the responsibility of Child-rearing. And I am well aware that many will feel my views and opinions are antiquated or old-fashioned, but they point to the proper order of life in Christ. "I say therefore to the unmarried and widows, it is good for them if they abide even as I. 9 But if they cannot contain, let them marry: for it is better to marry than to burn. 10 And unto the married I command, yet not I, but the Lord, Let not the wife depart from her husband:" (1 Corinthians 7:8-10). Have you noticed, because of the Internet and certain Therapeutics, man has managed to slow his Natural Biological Clock. And this has caused our father's and grandfather's normal Mid-life Crisis to go into extra innings. Remember, God did not preserve and keep us through our terrible twenties only to lose us in what should be our faithful fifties. As the final stages of our lives begin, we should have reached the point where we are fully committed to pleasing God. "So then they that are in the flesh cannot please God." (Romans 8:8). One of the main differences between the Kingdom of Heaven and the Kingdom of Men is that you do not age out of the Kingdom of Heaven. In the Kingdom of Men, everyone has a shelf life. Once we reach a certain age in the Kingdom of Men, regardless of Fame or Occupation, we begin to lose value. And, it becomes quite evident when this occurs because people will lose interest and have little use or time for yesterday's Hero. Movie actors that were big box-office stars in their twenties can barely find a desirable part to play when they reach sixty. A sports franchise built on the Athletic abilities of one of the greatest players ever to play the game, will remove that player from the team Roster when he fails to produce another Championship.

A fifty-year-old employee who has decades of experience, but lost his job because the Plant moved overseas, will have trouble finding a suitable position because others will feel he is too old for employment.

It is the opposite in the Kingdom of Heaven; you can be of more use and have greater value in your mature years. The tried-and-true wisdom and maturity gained from your Christian experiences can help the younger generation find and stay on the proper path of righteousness. You still have worth. "But speak thou the things which become sound doctrine: 2 That the aged men be sober, grave, temperate, sound in faith, in charity, in patience. 3 The aged women likewise, that they be in behaviour as becometh holiness, not false accusers, not given to much wine, teachers of good things; 4 That they may teach the young women to be sober, to love their husbands, to love their children," (Titus 2:1-4). "Hear, O my son, and receive my sayings; and the years of thy life shall be many. 11 I have taught thee in the way of wisdom; I have led thee in right paths." (Proverbs 4:10-11). As it was alluded to by these scriptures, those of us who have aged and grown in the wisdom of God still have a vital role to play within the Kingdom of Heaven. We must continue to tell the generations that follow us, our grandchildren and their children, that Jesus is the only Way. And yes, I know you are wearied and worn. And it seems like a lost cause. Because your once beautiful grandchild now has a face tattoo or large holes through her ear lobes called gauges. I know you think he wears his pants too low, and she always wears her skirts way too high. And even if that grandchild is living as part of a Throuple or some other alternative lifestyle, you must keep speaking the truth because you know God is able. "I have been young, and now am old; yet have I not seen the righteous forsaken, nor his seed begging bread. 26 He is ever merciful, and lendeth; and his seed is blessed." (Psalm 37:25-26).

The lust of the eyes is one of the cornerstones in which the Kingdom of Men is built. In other words, they will not believe it unless they see it. "He saved others; himself he cannot save.

If he be the King of Israel, let him now come down from the cross, and we will believe him." (Matthew 27:42). "Then said Jesus unto him, Except ye see signs and wonders, ye will not believe." (John 4:48). And whatever a man sees he wants. Have you ever become disenchanted with your blessing after observing a known sinner that seems to have more than you? "Rest in the Lord, and wait patiently for him: fret not thyself because of him who prospereth in his way, because of the man who bringeth wicked devices to pass." (Psalm 37:7). My mother had a couple of sayings about that, especially when I would start to feel unhappy about my own circumstances. First, "Everything that glitters isn't gold," and everything that looks good to you may not be good for you". Never have two statements been so true, specifically when you consider how we got into this mess in the first place. "And when the woman saw that the tree was good for food, and that it was pleasant to the eyes, and a tree to be desired to make one wise, she took of the fruit thereof, and did eat, and gave also unto her husband with her; and he did eat." (Genesis 3:6). In the Kingdom of Heaven sight is not as important as faith. "(For we walk by faith, not by sight:)." (2 Corinthians 5:7).

After mentioning gold, this brings me to another point as it relates to the differences between the Kingdom of Heaven and the Kingdom of Men. This point will also segue into the Pride of Life as well. The preeminent currency in the Kingdom of Men is gold, but not so in the Kingdom of Heaven. The only currency in the Kingdom of Heaven is faith, and it is so important that it is impossible to please our God without it. "But without faith it is impossible to please him: for he that cometh to God must believe that he is, and that he is a rewarder of them that diligently seek him." (Hebrews 11:6). Take Caleb and Joshua; they did not purchase their land with silver and gold, no, they purchased it with their faith. "And Joshua blessed him, and gave unto Caleb the son of Jephunneh Hebron for an inheritance." (Joshua 14:13). "When they had made an end of dividing the land for inheritance by their coasts, the children of Israel gave an inheritance to

Joshua the son of Nun among them: 50 According to the word of the Lord they gave him the city which he asked, even Timnathserah in mount Ephraim: and he built the city, and dwelt therein." (Joshua 19:49-50). Also, in the Kingdom of Heaven, since faith is the only currency, then love is the Bank that guarantees the Note. And there is a branch open near you. "In this was manifested the love of God toward us, because that God sent his only begotten Son into the world, that we might live through him. 10 Herein is love, not that we loved God, but that he loved us, and sent his Son to be the propitiation for our sins. 11 Beloved, if God so loved us, we ought also to love one another." (1 John 4:9-11). "A new commandment I give unto you, That ye love one another; as I have loved you, that ye also love one another. 35 By this shall all men know that ye are my disciples, if ye have love one to another." (John 13:34-35). The Kingdom of Men is driven by wealth and power; with wealth and power comes titles and possessions, which brings about Pride. Because of who I am and what I have, I am better than you. I am a god among men; this is the status quo of the Kingdom of Men. But always remember, no matter what you Pride yourself in, you can be somebody today and a nobody tomorrow. "Charge them that are rich in this world, that they be not highminded, nor trust in uncertain riches, but in the living God, who giveth us richly all things to enjoy;" (1 Timothy 6:17).

There are billions upon billions of stories of how each of us got to this moment. As a collective on our journey, some have found great fame and wealth on the Mountain Top, and others have rested in the Valley. Some have built the Wonders of the World, and yet others have destroyed Empires. Some are at peace on the Sea, while others worship the Land. From my studies, prayer, and spiritual discernment, I pronounce that all the Roads we travel in life only lead to two places. No matter who you are and what you have or have not accomplished, all Roads lead to Heaven or Hell.

"We took sweet counsel together, and walked unto the house of God in company. 15 Let death seize upon them, and let them go down quick into hell: for wickedness is in their dwellings, and among them. 16 As for me, I will call upon God; and the Lord shall save me." (Psalm 55:14-16). With this understanding, one can deduce if the roads through the Kingdom of Heaven lead to God, then by default, the roads through the Kingdom of Men lead to Hell. "There is a way that seemeth right unto a man, but the end thereof are the ways of death." (Proverbs 16:25). Satan has designed this world with one goal in mind. To put it simply, the world with which Man is most comfortable is designed to send him straight to Hell. And if you manage to get out alive through Christ, Satan will do his damnedest to ensure you will not help others get into Heaven. I beg you, while amid hatred and doubt, do not let this world shape you or your behavior. Satan is holding and molding you if you are not held safe in the Potter's Hands. "Then the word of the Lord came to me, saying, 6 O house of Israel, cannot I do with you as this potter? saith the Lord. Behold, as the clay is in the potter's hand, so are ye in mine hand, O house of Israel." (Jeremiah 18:5-6). Please, brothers and sisters, you must remain ever Vigilant. This world is fool's gold; none of it is real. It is all an illusion created by Satan; if you allow any of the things of this world to seep into your consciousness, all is lost. "A little leaven leaveneth the whole lump." (Galatians 5:9). Here are some of the statements that this sinful world lives by. "Looking out for number one." "The ends justify the means." "Nice guys finish last." "Kill or be killed," "Dog eat dog" and "Only the strong survive." I would also like to add that if you have learned life's lessons at the school of hard knocks, you, my friend had a poor education. If you live by a Code that is not written in the Word of God, then it's written on the walls of Hell. Do you know someone who always seems to be angry with the world? They say things like, "I'm mad as hell, and I am not going to take it anymore."

If you answer yes to any of those questions for anyone you may know, it means Satan's system has a stronghold in that person's life. Unknowingly this will cause the individual to lose or damage his Testimony. Please consider how can a person testify to others about the goodness of God and say that God is love when they are always mad at something or someone. "Ye cannot drink the cup of the Lord, and the cup of devils: ye cannot be partakers of the Lord's table, and of the table of devils." (1 Corinthians 10:21). Many people are unaware of how important their testimony can be. Testimony is the Gravity that grounds us in the Kingdom of Heaven. According to the scripture, the power of someone's testimony will play an integral part in the End Times. I will go into greater detail about this in the next chapter; The End Is Near.

Just as Jesus was committed to his Father's business, we must remain committed to that cause. Unfortunately, most men know more Sports stats than Bible verses. They pride themselves in that knowledge, unaware that one day they must stand before the Lord and give an account. And trust me, the Most High will not be interested in who scored the most points in a game, nor which team has the most championship titles. "For it is written, As I live, saith the Lord, every knee shall bow to me, and every tongue shall confess to God. 12 So then every one of us shall give account of himself to God." (Romans 14:11-12). We as Men cling to and rely more on our Male Masculinity than Jesus. The Kingdom of Men introduces violent behavior to children at an early age. They teach their sons never to run from a fight; if someone hits you, hit them back. I have seen boys grow into men who have lived by this code all their lives; trust me, it did not serve them well. Most continue to fight in and out of Jail. Do you honestly believe the God we serve would care about how many times you stood your ground as a real Man and fought without reserve? When you fight for any cause other than the cause of Christ, you may not know it, but you are already defeated.

I hope these writings will help our beloved sisters who struggle through doubt, hatred, sexism, and abuse in the Kingdom of Men. Today's society embraces a deceptive bag of images for women, indecent, brash, and free-spirited. These vibrant descriptions are now considered normal. Our teenage daughters, our sisters, and in many cases, our mothers openly exploit their Sexuality. The Internet is inundated with explicit photos and videos of women. Statistically, most women are motivated by the ever elusive and trending "Like" in this attention-driven economy. This type of behavior can be detrimental to your Mental and Physical well-being. Please understand, the attention you garner from men is fleeting at best; at its worst, it can be deadly. "Every wise woman buildeth her house: but the foolish plucketh it down with her hands." (Proverbs 14:1). Whether woman or man it does not matter, we truly cannot allow Satan and the Kingdom of Men to continue to fool us. We must watch, wait, and guard our Hearts for the glory of the Kingdom of Heaven.

"Keep thy heart with all diligence; for out of it are the issues of life." (Proverbs 4:23).

Chapter Ten

THE END IS NEAR

"For as the lightning cometh out of the east, and shineth even unto the west; so shall also the coming of the Son of man be. 40 Then shall two be in the field; the one shall be taken, and the other left. 41 Two women shall be grinding at the mill; the one shall be taken, and the other left. 42 Watch therefore: for ye know not what hour your Lord doth come." (Matthew 24:27,40-42).

As you may have noticed, I have talked to you as my friends throughout the book, and this chapter will be no different. In this way, we have perused and pondered together the condition of the Faith. As I move forward writing this chapter, I will not back my statements with references from the many journals or articles that reinforce my observations as truth. Rather, I will write plainly in the hope that you will reflect and parallel your thoughts with my own. In this last chapter, I can now confess the reason for the book. These are my ten personal conventions for faith shared, projected, and professed for my friends, loved ones, and legacy. This is my final proposition to propel your faith in our Lord and Savior. We have finally arrived at the last chapter of this my first book, titled "The End Is Near." I would guess that deep down inside, we all knew those guys standing on the street corners proclaiming "the End is Near" would eventually be proven right. And, according to Bible prophecy, together, we have trodden the path to our End Days, signified for us Believers by the Imminent return of Christ Jesus. "And as he sat upon the mount of Olives, the disciples came unto him privately, saying, Tell us, when shall these things be? and what shall be the sign of thy coming, and of the end of the world? 4 And Jesus answered and said unto them,

Take heed that no man deceive you. 5 For many shall come in my name, saying, I am Christ; and shall deceive many. 6 And ye shall hear of wars and rumors of wars: see that ye be not troubled: for all these things must come to pass, but the end is not yet. 7 For nation shall rise against nation, and kingdom against kingdom: and there shall be famines, and pestilences, and earthquakes, in divers places. 8 All these are the beginning of sorrows. 9 Then shall they deliver you up to be afflicted, and shall kill you: and ye shall be hated of all nations for my name's sake. 10 And then shall many be offended, and shall betray one another, and shall hate one another. 11 And many false prophets shall rise, and shall deceive many. 12 And because iniquity shall abound, the love of many shall wax cold. 13 But he that shall endure unto the end, the same shall be saved." (Matthew 24:3-13).

This teaching of Jesus' return is called the Olivet Discourse. This Discourse is also found in the other Synoptic Gospels: Mark chapter 13 and Luke chapter 21. Let us take a closer look at the Olivet Discourse and ascertain how many of Jesus' prophecies have come to pass and what remains to be revealed to us. Based on my research, we can check off all the boxes except one. Oddly enough, it is the first proclamation of the prophecy. Be not deceived many individuals will come and claim to be the Christ. Over the years there have been some twisted people or crackpots claiming to be the Messiah or Son of God. In my opinion, no one of any significance has emerged claiming to be Christ the Savior. No one as of yet has satisfied the necessary requirement of the Christ. So, as it stands, the Antichrist is the only shoe that remains to drop. I will examine the signs of his arrival shortly, but first, let us continue with the rest of the prophecies from the Olivet Discourse. Wars and rumors of Wars are thus demonstrable. Currently, several wars are raging around the globe, and I do not doubt that there are more to follow. America just recently ended its war in Afghanistan which lasted twenty years.

And we may get dragged into a conflict with China over Taiwan. Because China is loudly threatening to reclaim Taiwan by force if necessary. America has promised to protect Taiwan at all costs. One could easily think that with our collective intelligence and technological advancements, humans could find some other way than the brutal actions of War to resolve our issues. Nations are against nations: Russia is surely against Ukraine, China is against Taiwan, Hamas is against Israel, and India is against Pakistan, to name just a few impending conflicts. And with these wars and confrontations, along with global climate change and widespread natural disasters. Permanent food shortages have been reported worldwide. This means we can also check off Famine from our list of prophecies. The Pestilences statement goes without saying. It was announced in 2022 by the World Health Organization that the Corona Virus had claimed six million lives Globally. Experts recommend we wipe our package with disinfectant to kill the undetectable virus. And we have all seen the devastating effects of earthquakes in diverse places like Haiti, Indonesia, Nepal, etc.

Many Theologians believe the first part of verse 9 from the Olivet Discourse in Matthew; - they shall kill you - was committed during the persecution period of the early Church by Saul and the Jews, as well as by Nero and the Romans. Here in modern times, Russia has banned the Jehovah's Witness Church from conducting services within their country. Also, because of this governmental action, Jehovah's Witnesses are persecuted and turned over to Russian authorities for practicing their Faith. Remember, verse 9 also states all Nations will hate us because we are followers of Christ. Hate is such a fickle word to describe the treatment of Christians by the world, but I believe Hate is the most absolute and accurate description. Today if you do say you are a Christian, people will immediately think you are sexist, intolerant, homophobic, a con artist, or a hypocrite. Are not all these descriptions just metaphors for capturing the pure hate the world has for Christianity? For instance, there is a stain on the largest denomination within the Christian Faith, the Catholic Church. The public has become disappointed with the Church because of the many Sexual Abuse Scandals brought forward recently. It was disheartening to learn about the poor treatment the victims suffered at the hands of the Church's leadership and the lack of punishment given to their abusers. The reputation of the Catholic Church and Christianity, in general, has suffered a devastating blow because of many other scandals as well. Today many speak ill of the Faith because they believe Christians are void of any and all Integrity. I am sure we all offer our prayers to those who have suffered abuse at the hands of any within the Faith. Like many Christians striving to follow our Lord daily, I hope you find peace and solace. Also, many Christian volunteers are being tortured and killed in some countries because of the name of Christ, while others are kidnapped and held for ransom.

And simultaneously, as you may have seen, the atrocities against Christians are too numerous to count. But what is truly troubling is the amount of discord within the Christian Faith. Consider the many Denominations that have formed due to disagreements. These actions help satisfy verse 10. Also, new-age Religions are on the rise in many countries around the world. They twist the scriptures and subvert Holy doctrine to fit their narratives. And, many of these New Church leaders refer to themselves as Prophets, which by default checks off verse 11. Also, it goes without saying; love is a human emotion that is rarely practiced in our cold and heartless society. True examples of Brotherly love are few and far between. Consider the Holiday Season, for instance. It is not uncommon for families to fight at the Thanksgiving Dinner table, and these loving relatives are not fighting over a keepsake or an unfairly divided Inheritance. No, it is over something far more objectionable, Politics. And please consider this offense toward the Holiday Spirit? Every year some unfortunate soul will be trampled to death at a Black Friday Sale. While others are robbed at gunpoint in the Mall's parking lot.

Hear me and hear me well. There is a discernible change in the Spiritual Atmosphere. For instance, consider the unnecessary violence occurring on our Nation's Highways. Because of Road Rage, innocent children have lost their lives riding in the back seat of their parent's car. What could cause such non-empathetic behavior? Surely you understand; if God is Love, then Hate and Anger are of the Devil. Satan will take a minor disagreement between you and your neighbor over something as innocent as a fence and turn it into an incident you will regret for the rest of your days. I beg you, turn the other cheek by walking away. Once again, Satan will use your Male Masculinity against you. The Devil knows what trigger words anger you. Consider how many altercations have started with an overtly aggressive statement. Please stop falling for these tricks of the enemy.

Now let me address the signs of the Antichrist. The entity, human being, or spirit poised to oppose the coming of Christ by any tactic or strategy it deems necessary. The term Antichrist appears in the King James Bible four times, all in the Epistles of John. However, he is also referenced in several other books of the Bible: Daniel, Zechariah, 2 Thessalonians, and yes, Revelations. There are some in society that believe the Antichrist lives among us presently. They believe he is waiting for the right opportunity or catastrophe before he reveals himself. I myself do not believe he has been born yet. If he has, which I seriously doubt, he would currently be an Infant. A significant part of my beliefs is based on his Pedigree. The Antichrist must fulfill all of the Messianic Prophecies, which I will not list here because there are many. At least thirty as a low estimate, and possibly over two hundred as a high estimate, which is contingent upon which scriptures you choose to interpret and your Methodology. Case in point, here is one of the many Prophecies on which I base my beliefs of the Antichrist not being born yet. The Antichrist would have to be born of a Virgin, just as Jesus was born of the Virgin Mary, his Mother.

Once you consider we live in the age of the World Wide Web, a place where the most mundane information is shared over and over again. The advent of a Child born onto a Virgin without the presence of a Man would break the Internet. Would it not? Here is another key fact about the Antichrist that supports my position. The prophecy that states the Antichrist will defile the Temple of our God. "Let no man deceive you by any means: for that day shall not come, except there come a falling away first, and that man of sin be revealed, the son of perdition; 4 Who opposeth and exalteth himself above all that is called God, or that is worshipped; so that he as God sitteth in the temple of God, shewing himself that he is God." (2 Thessalonians 2:3-4). The Temple that stood in Jesus' time was destroyed in 70 A.D. by the Romans. This means a new Temple must be built before this particular prophecy could come to pass. Which would be highly unlikely; because there is a structure currently on the site, The Dome of the Rock. The Dome of the Rock is one of Islam's holiest sites. It was built in 685 A.D, and it is where Muslims believe their Prophet Muhammad ascended into Heaven. The Dome of the Rock is located on the Temple Mount, and to further complicate the matter, some Jewish Theologians believe it stands on the very spot where the Holy of Holies was once located. All Christians know the Holy of Holies is where the presence of God would reside when He came into His Temple. The only person allowed to enter into the Holy of Holies when God was present was the High Priest. So, here's the situation. For the Temple to be rebuilt, Jews and Muslims would have to agree on relocating the Dome of the Rock. And when you consider they have not agreed on little or nothing in the past seventy years, it is doubtful that will change in the immediate future. If Israel attempts to do it without an agreement with its Muslim neighbors, it would most certainly bring about a Holy War with Islam. So, what can we conclude? There are currently no official plans to rebuild the Temple. And if there were, the Global community would not allow it.

In the interim, we cannot afford to sit idly by and wait for the inevitable evil that will come to pass one day. We must take up our noble cause and do as Paul Revere did on that fateful day. Warn our fellow Man to heed the times and take up Spiritual Arms for evil approaches. I must admit, I myself never took those guys standing on the street corners with The End Is Near signs seriously. That is until now. The events of the last three decades have convinced me to heed their ominous message. What I truly find troubling is I am not late to the End is Near party; I am actually early. How can this be? People, we are at DEFCON 1. The return of Christ is Imminent, and the Battle of Armageddon is a certainty. At this moment, only a few Christians have shown any interest in preparing for these events. Let me provide some context, I travel weekly, and it is not uncommon to see someone running into the airport to catch their flight. On certain occasions, I have had to move quickly to my gate. The P.A. announcement about final boarding can be quite motivating. As travelers, we react and change our behavior when we know that time is running out.

Hear me and hear me well, people. Time is running out, and we need to change our behavior, for the End is truly Near! Please, my fellow Believers, we must surely govern ourselves accordingly because Hell is real. And unlike us, Hell is making the necessary arrangements to accommodate those who will fall short when judged by Jesus upon his return. "Hell from beneath is moved for thee to meet thee at thy coming: it stirreth up the dead for thee, even all the chief ones of the earth; it hath raised up from their thrones all the kings of the nations." (Isaiah 14:9). If you want to know how to govern yourself accordingly, I can explain the term using my travel experiences. When I travel to unfamiliar places, I do my research. I consult google maps for the destination in which I am visiting. When I arrive at the airport, I look for signage (e.g., rental car, hotel shuttles, light rail). Dear readers, please do your research. For we are truly sailing in uncharted waters through a foreign land.

"Study to shew thyself approved unto God, a workman that needeth not to be ashamed, rightly dividing the word of truth." (2 Timothy 2:15).

Now, having done your research and made the necessary preparations. You will discover, as I have discovered, that Jesus is not actually returning for the Church as we know it. "Not every one that saith unto me, Lord, Lord, shall enter into the kingdom of heaven; but he that doeth the will of my Father which is in heaven. 22 Many will say to me in that day, Lord, Lord, have we not prophesied in thy name? and in thy name have cast out devils? and in thy name done many wonderful works? 23 And then will I profess unto them, I never knew you: depart from me, ye that work iniquity." (Matthew 7:21-23). Before you label me, a sinful Blasphemer and burn my book, allow me time to explain. These scriptures speak about parishioners who attend Church regularly. People that we may respect and admire. Individuals who may hold positions of authority and power within the Church (e.g., Pastor, Bishop, Deacon, Trustee) and laypeople who have sat in the pews for decades. The Church that Jesus Christ is returning for is the one he bought with his Blood, the one true Church that belongs to God. "What? know ye not that your body is the temple of the Holy Ghost which is in you, which ye have of God, and ye are not your own? 20 For ye are bought with a price: therefore glorify God in your body, and in your spirit, which are God's." (1 Corinthians 6:19-20). Simply put, Jesus is coming back for those who are indwelled with the Holy Spirit. If you are born of the Blood of Jesus and are in true relationship with God, you are Saved. Congratulation, Jesus is coming back for you.

In these last days, we must cease and desist with Man-made Religious Dogma. Stop it; no one is going to Hell because they choose to worship on a certain day. Nor is Heaven denied to someone because they were sprinkled with water as a child and not submerged in a Baptismal Pool. Also, some denominations believe a Blood Transfusion could condemn a person's Soul.

What nonsense, a blood transfusion cannot affect a person's Soul. No medical procedure can do this. A blood transfusion cannot save your life. At best, it may prolong the life you already have. The only blood that can give or save a life is the Blood of Jesus. "Then Jesus said unto them, Verily, verily, I say unto you, Except ye eat the flesh of the Son of man, and drink his blood, ye have no life in you." (John 6:53). Also, your Father God is not going to deny you - His Child - access to Heaven because you believe, or do not believe, He is part of a Trinity. Do you believe we feeble humans can add to or diminish God? How foolish are those that think they fully understand any facet of the Creator - He is that He is. "Then the Lord answered Job out of the whirlwind, and said, 2 Who is this that darkeneth counsel by words without knowledge? 3 Gird up now thy loins like a man; for I will demand of thee, and answer thou me. 4 Where wast thou when I laid the foundations of the earth? declare, if thou hast understanding." (Job 38:1-4). My fellow Believers, stop trying to deny access into Heaven to followers of Jesus who do not worship as you do. These fragmented, fractured, opinionated beliefs and concoctions are part of that Brainwashing I mention in chapter 7, The Power of The Tongue. These are just a few examples of how the Devil sows discord. Satan is using you to further confuse those who do not know the Lord or are new to the Faith.

Here is another case in point. Some denominations teach against Christmas and the Christmas Tree. They need to regain their Spiritual focus. Christmas and a Christmas Tree are no more evil than Super Bowl Sunday and your television. They teach that we are purposely spreading a lie when we say Jesus was born on December 25th; that concoction could not be further from the truth. You must offer definitive proof to prove something is a lie. And since no one knows for certain the day of Jesus' birth, who can say with all confidence, that it is not the 25th of December? ever, if we are speaking of probabilities, I would agree that gher likelihood that Jesus was not born on December 25th.

Truth be told, the actual date of his birth is not as important as the day you were Born Again. And, if you have been Born Again, you should understand we are not spreading a lie. To lie is to deceive, and we are not spreading deception. We are spreading love - the love of Christ. To a true Born-Again Believer, every day is Christmas. I celebrate the birth of Jesus every day of the year and give gifts of joy and good tidings to all I meet. "And the angel said unto them, Fear not: for, behold, I bring you good tidings of great joy, which shall be to all people. 11 For unto you is born this day in the city of David a Saviour, which is Christ the Lord." (Luke 2:10-11). Also, let us not forget the spiritual draw that Christmas has on some nonbelievers. It truly has become a tremendous Evangelizing resource for Christianity. After all, you have to say Christ to say Christmas, and there is power in the precious name of Christ. The name of Christ has converted many nonbelievers who attended Church service on Christmas Day.

Now to address this nonsense concerning the Christmas Tree. And yes, I know what the Bible says about Decorating a Tree. "Thus saith the Lord, Learn not the way of the heathen, and be not dismayed at the signs of heaven; for the heathen are dismayed at them. 3 For the customs of the people are vain: for one cutteth a tree out of the forest, the works of the hands of the workman, with the axe. 4 They deck it with silver and with gold; they fasten it with nails and with hammers, that it move not." (Jeremiah 10:2-4). Starting with verse 2, "at the signs of heaven." This scripture describes astronomical events and the actions ancient people would take when they saw a Comet or a Lunar Eclipse. Naturally, these rarely seen anomalies would frighten the observers, after which their fears would cause them to make an offering to their pagan gods with "the works of the hands," verse 3. This is an obvious indication of a workman's hands-on craftsmanship. This scripture clearly describes how these ancient cultures would create, decorate, and worship idols made from the trees they cut from the forest. And they hoped this would appease their angry gods.

This type of woodwork resembles the totem poles that early Native American cultures would create. They are also similar to those you have seen in Egyptian and Greek Mythology. And none of these idols resemble what we know of as a Christmas Tree. Also, I have never heard or seen anyone make an offering to or worship a Christmas Tree. We must never study the scriptures for the sole purpose of only identifying what we believe are other followers' shortcomings. "And why beholdest thou the mote that is in thy brother's eye, but perceivest not the beam that is in thine own eye? 42 Either how canst thou say to thy brother, Brother, let me pull out the mote that is in thine eye, when thou thyself beholdest not the beam that is in thine own eye? Thou hypocrite, cast out first the beam out of thine own eye, and then shalt thou see clearly to pull out the mote that is in thy brother's eye." (Luke 6:41-42). Remember, the Pharisees thought they were righteous as well. This is what Satan does.

These types of Demonic tactics have caused us to divide God's beloved Church into hundreds of denominations in the United States and over thousands upon thousands Globally. All of which are mostly teaching against the other. We must put an end to this type of behavior. Jesus addressed this very matter with the Disciples. "And John answered and said, Master, we saw one casting out devils in thy name; and we forbad him, because he followeth not with us. 50 And Jesus said unto him, Forbid him not: for he that is not against us is for us." (Luke 9:49-50). Children of God, please remember what was stated earlier in Matthew chapter 24, verse 9. Our enemies are coming for us all. Satan and his minions seek to destroy anyone who calls on the name of the Lord, regardless of religion or denomination. Do you honestly believe the Devil will come for the Catholics and leave the Methodists? Do you think he will kill the Baptist and let the Mormons live? Are you of the opinion that Satan will burn down a Church of Christ and let the Kingdom Hall stand? If you are, you are sadly mistaken.

Hear me and hear me well. If Jesus Christ, the Son of God, is the foundation of your Religious Faith, then that Faith is sealed in the body of Christ. "Therefore thus saith the Lord God, Behold, I lay in Zion for a foundation a stone, a tried stone, a precious corner stone, a sure foundation: he that believeth shall not make haste." (Isaiah 28:16). "And Simon Peter answered and said, Thou art the Christ, the Son of the living God. 18 And I say also unto thee, That thou art Peter, and upon this rock I will build my church; and the gates of hell shall not prevail against it." (Matthew 16:16,18). Once again, if you truly love the Lord and are born again, you are Saved, and let no Demon in Hell tell you otherwise.

Back to the return of Christ. I understand why the second coming of Christ is not newsworthy to the media. However, I do not understand why it is not trending in the faith-based community. The second coming of Jesus Christ should be the topic of every Sunday Sermon, every Bible Study, and every Book written by a Believer. Every Pastor and every Christian, should be declaring the message of Jesus' return from their rooftops. I know some Believers may be a little reluctant to do so because we cannot give a definite day and date for the return of our Messiah. But according to scripture, that is by God's design. No one knows the exact time of Christ's return, not even Jesus himself; only God knows. "But of that day and that hour knoweth no man, no, not the angels which are in heaven, neither the Son, but the Father. 33 Take ye heed, watch and pray: for ye know not when the time is." (Mark 13:32-33).

Earlier in chapter 3, Collateral Damage, I mentioned that Satan was not all-knowing. But he certainly knows three things: the who, what, and why of Jesus Christ. "And there was in their synagogue a man with an unclean spirit; and he cried out, 24 Saying, Let us alone; what have we to do with thee, thou Jesus of Nazareth? art thou come to destroy us? I know thee who thou art, the Holy One of God" (Mark 1:23-24).

Satan knew the coming of Jesus would signal the beginning of the end of his reign here on earth. That is why he tried to kill the Messiah as an infant. "Now when Jesus was born in Bethlehem of Judaea in the days of Herod the king, behold, there came wise men from the east to Jerusalem, 2 Saying, Where is he that is born King of the Jews? for we have seen his star in the east, and are come to worship him. 3 When Herod the king had heard these things, he was troubled, and all Jerusalem with him. 4 And when he had gathered all the chief priests and scribes of the people together, he demanded of them where Christ should be born. 5 And they said unto him, In Bethlehem of Judaea: for thus it is written by the prophet, 11 And when they were come into the house, they saw the young child with Mary his mother, and fell down, and worshipped him: and when they had opened their treasures, they presented unto him gifts; gold, and frankincense and myrrh. 13 And when they were departed, behold, the angel of the Lord appeareth to Joseph in a dream, saying, Arise, and take the young child and his mother, and flee into Egypt, and be thou there until I bring thee word: for Herod will seek the young child to destroy him. 14 When he arose, he took the young child and his mother by night, and departed into Egypt: 15 And was there until the death of Herod: that it might be fulfilled which was spoken of the Lord by the prophet, saying, Out of Egypt have I called my son. 16 Then Herod, when he saw that he was mocked of the wise men, was exceeding wroth, and sent forth, and slew all the children that were in Bethlehem, and in all the coasts thereof, from two years old and under, according to the time which he had diligently inquired of the wise men." (Matthew 2:1-5,11,13-16). So, if the Messiah's first coming signal to Satan the beginning of his end. Then, it stands to reason that Satan knows the Messiah's second coming is his end. The Bible showed us how Satan did everything within his power to stop the Messiah from being born. The Bible also states that in the last days, Satan will do everything within his power to lengthen his days. And by doing so, slow the return of Jesus.

But glory be to God; according to scripture, the Lord will not allow Satan to trouble His Children indefinitely. "For in those days shall be affliction, such as was not from the beginning of the creation which God created unto this time, neither shall be. 20 And except that the Lord had shortened those days, no flesh should be saved: but for the elect's sake, whom he hath chosen, he hath shortened the days. 21 And then if any man shall say to you, Lo, here is Christ; or, lo, he is there; believe him not: 22 For false Christs and false prophets shall rise, and shall shew signs and wonders, to seduce, if it were possible, even the elect. 23 But take ye heed: behold, I have foretold you all things." (Mark 13:19-23).

I can remember when my children were little, and a storm would arrive. At the first sound of thunder, I would hear the sounds of their little feet running all over the house. Searching for me - their father. And when they finally found me, usually resting on the couch. My children would leap into my arms, trembling with fear, and ask me if everything would be alright. I would console them and proclaim to my son and daughter that everything would be fine. Because the Lord and I would always protect them and keep them from harm. Feeling safe, they would eventually fall asleep in my arms, knowing God had us covered. What is my point? In these last days, we must not panic, running to and fro because of the storms of life. We must seek out Jesus and when we find him, rest in his arms, knowing God has us covered. "And to you who are troubled rest with us, when the Lord Jesus shall be revealed from heaven with his mighty angels," (2 Thessalonians 1:7).

Earlier, I said some of us may be reluctant to spread the word of Jesus' return because we do not know the day or the date. I have found a solution to that obstacle. My research has shown me when Jesus will return. Howbeit, I do not know the day and date because it was never predicated on a day and date. The second coming of Jesus Christ is predicated on an event, not a date. Let me explain how I came to this conclusion.

Recently I asked my mentor to provide me with a list of what he thought were the ten most important scriptures related to Man. He responded they all are important because the Bible is the fixed word of God. And while I do respect him, and I do understand his response to not favor one scripture over another. My research has shown me that some scriptures are more vital to Man than others. Let's consult the Bible on this crucial matter. For this demonstration, I have chosen two random scriptures. The first represents a vital scripture as it relates to Man, and the second is pleasing to the ear but less vital. First, "For the grace of God that bringeth salvation hath appeared to all men," (Titus 2:11). This would be considered a vital scripture; it tells us Jesus has made salvation available to every man. Second, "And all the days of Methuselah were nine hundred sixty and nine years: and he died." (Genesis 5:27). This scripture tells us Methuselah almost lived to be a thousand. Very interesting, but not vitally important. I hope you see my point. My position is not unfounded. The Bible also shows us Jesus himself reduced the 613 Mosaic Laws down to what he said were the two most important. "Master, which is the great commandment in the law? 37 Jesus said unto him, Thou shalt love the Lord thy God with all thy heart, and with all thy soul, and with all thy mind. 38 This is the first and great commandment. 39 And the second is like unto it, Thou shalt love thy neighbour as thyself. 40 On these two commandments hang all the law and the prophets." (Matthew 22:36-40).

So, with this understanding, here are the ten scriptures I found to be vitally important to the condition of Man. And most importantly, be aware that one of the ten will play a role in the second coming of our Lord and Savior, Jesus Christ. Our future with God is spelled out in the book of Revelation, but to better understand this, we must look to the beginning - Genesis. In the book of Genesis, we will find 4 of my ten most vital scriptures.

My first vital scripture is, "And the Lord God formed man of the dust of the ground, and breathed into his nostrils the breath of life; and man became a living soul." (Genesis 2:7). This is truly a beautiful and amazing scripture. God desired to share His Creation with someone other than Himself. So, He created Man, and unlike anything else in Creation, Man had a Soul. And God loved Man so much that He created a companion to share the beauty of Creation with him. God knew it was not good for Man to be alone.

My second vital scripture is, "And the rib, which the Lord God had taken from man, made he a woman, and brought her unto the man." (Genesis 2:22). It is here in this verse that we can envision what God initially attended for Man and Woman. It was unity, unity with each other, and unity with Him. Unfortunately, the unity God shared with Man would soon be broken.

My Third vital scripture is, "And when the woman saw that the tree was good for food, and that it was pleasant to the eyes, and a tree to be desired to make one wise, she took of the fruit thereof, and did eat, and gave also unto her husband with her; and he did eat." (Genesis 3:6). This scripture is truly foundational. Mostly everything written in the Bible after Genesis 3 verse 6 is mainly instruction on how Man could regain fellowship with God his Creator. Following Adam and Eve's removal from the Garden, they began to multiply in numbers and also in Sin. And because of the continuation of sin, God decided to destroy Man and remove him from the face of the Earth.

My fourth vital scripture is, "But Noah found grace in the eyes of the Lord." (Genesis 6:8). God decided that if Man were to remain on the Earth and Spiritually prosper, he would need help. So, God provided Man with written Instruction on how to accomplish what was desired of him.

My fifth vital scripture is, "This book of the law shall not depart out of thy mouth; but thou shalt meditate therein day and night, that thou mayest observe to do according to all that is written therein: for then thou shalt make thy way prosperous, and then thou shalt have good success." (Joshua 1:8). In the fullness of time, God sent forth Christ to redeem Man.

My sixth vital scripture is, "For God so loved the world, that he gave his only begotten Son, that whosoever believeth in him should not perish, but have everlasting life." (John 3:16). For Jesus Christ to completely redeem Man, he would have to pay the ultimate price. Jesus would have to die on the Cross at Calvary for Man's Sins. However, not only would Jesus have to die for Man's sins, he could not remain dead. Jesus would also have to rise from death as Justification that he was the Messiah.

My seventh vital scripture is, "And he saith unto them, Be not affrighted: Ye seek Jesus of Nazareth, which was crucified: he is risen; he is not here: behold the place where they laid him." (Mark 16:6). Having risen from the dead, Jesus has shown all Believers that death was not the end of life, only the beginning. There is a prepared place for prepared people. Jesus one day will return for God's Children so that we can spend Eternity with him and God.

My eighth vital scripture is, "And if I go and prepare a place for you, I will come again, and receive you unto myself; that where I am, there ye may be also." (John 14:3). Jesus also knew God's Children would need help in their preparation. Jesus prayed to the Father to send us a Comforter to teach and guide us, so God sent the Holy Spirit.

My ninth vital scripture is, "And they were all filled with the Holy Ghost, and began to speak with other tongues, as the Spirit gave them utterance." (Acts 2:4).

My friends, we have now arrived at the tenth scripture that is of Vital Importance to Man. It also serves as the Event that will close the door Adam opened and bring about the Return of Christ.

My tenth vital scripture is, "And this gospel of the kingdom shall be preached in all the world for a witness unto all nations; and then shall the end come." (Matthew 24:14).

There you have it, my brothers and sisters, the real reason you catch so much Hell in your life. Satan wants to destroy your ability to Testify about the Goodness of God. If Satan can cause you to lose your Testimony, you are not a threat to his kingdom. "Ye are the salt of the earth: but if the salt have lost his savour, wherewith shall it be salted? it is thenceforth good for nothing, but to be cast out, and to be trodden under foot of men." (Matthew 5:13). Satan knows at some point and place in time, a Child of God will Speak or Preach the Gospel to a person or a people who have yet to hear it. When they receive that last Gospel Message in their Heart. All as we know it shall come to an end, Hallelujah. The Trumpet will sound, the Clouds will roll up like a Scroll, and Jesus will descend from on High. Amen.

"For as a snare shall it come on all them that dwell on the face of the whole earth. 36 Watch ye therefore, and pray always, that ye may be accounted worthy to escape all these things that shall come to pass, and to stand before the Son of man." (Luke 21:35-36).

ACKNOWLEDGMENTS

First and foremost, I am the stereotypical only child, which means I am a Mama's boy. When I told my mother, I would start a church, she left her home church of forty years and became my first member. My mother, Evangelist Christine Sanders, truly loved the Lord and taught me to love the Lord as well. Any time I was in need of advice, she would quote Matthew chapter 6 verse 33; "But seek ye first the kingdom of God, and his righteousness; and all these things shall be added unto you." I still follow that advice today and I constantly advise her grandchildren to do the same. Sister Sanders believed in training a child in the ways he should go; when he's older, he will not depart. One of my fondest memory is when I left home for College, and she gave me her favorite Bible. Mom instructed me to read Matthew chapter 6, verse 33 if I ever needed help. That day eventually came, so, as she said, I got her Bible and turned to Matthew, and much to my surprise, there was a crisp hundred-dollar bill hidden between the pages. I cannot tell you what I spent the hundred dollars on, but I can tell you I still have her favorite Bible. It's a little worn now, but it still gets the job done. I Preach every one of my Sermons from it to this day. I also used it for research for this Book. I love and miss you, Mom, but I know you are Preaching and Praising all the day long in Heaven. Mom came by her faith honestly; her parents, James and Christina Brown, taught all their children about Jesus. And they practiced what they preached. We spent all Sunday in Church Service; Monday they would help clean the church, Wednesday they attended Bible Study, Thursday was Choir Rehearsal, and Saturday was Baptist Training Union. My grandparents' home was always welcoming, and often the air was filled with Gospel songs and the smell of freshly baked cakes.

They were always testifying about how good God had been to them. Thank you both for the history lessons and the love.

I was truly blessed when God selected my family for me. My mother had a sister Velma Lee Gaines; she was my aunt and mother. As I said, I was born an only child, but I never felt alone. My aunt Velma and her husband, Pastor E.L. Gaines had three children, and where ever they went, I went. The relationship I have with my brothers Rodney and Mark and our caring sister Ramona are ones that I cherish. And I dare not leave out Bridget. I love you guys.

My family was blessed with a true man of God, my uncle, Pastor E.L. Gaines. He was a man of few words, but when the subject changed to God and Pastoring, he was pretty vocal. His counsel and support have made me the man and preacher I am today. Pastor Gaines was one of the first Pastors to allow me to preach at his lovely Church. The Macedonia Missionary Baptist Church members continue to make me feel welcome and loved there. His guidance and instructions on being a husband, father, and Pastor are what directs me now. It is rare when a son-in-law becomes a son, which is what uncle Ernest became to my family. Velma Lee Brown chose well when she brought home this great man. Pastor Gaines, you are truly missed, but I know you can be found standing at the door of the house of the Lord, just as you said you would in a compelling Sermon I still remember to this day.
I look forward to that day when you open the door for me.

Just as Pastor Gaines taught me how to be a Pastor, I would have never become one if it were not for my Pastor, M.J. Johnson. Pastor Johnson saw what I did not see in myself when he chose me to serve on his Deacon Board. And later, God chose me to serve on the Pastor's staff. My many years at New Macedonia Missionary Baptist Church shaped my life.

I saw my grandmother serve as a Mother of the Church, and I was blessed to hear the many Sermons my mother delivered on Women's Day. What a joy it was, growing up in a Church that contained thirty of my family members at one time. It was a fantastic journey, transitioning from a child in the pews to a preacher in the pulpit. Pastor Johnson was the driving force behind all of this, and the greatest compliment he ever gave me was when he stopped calling me his member and started calling me his son. I miss you, dad.

To my current Pastor, Rodney Gaines. What can I say; you are my brother, friend, teacher, student, adviser, and confidant. It has been a joy to see you become the great man of God we all knew you were. Your honesty, wisdom, and humility are a rarity in today's Church. As we have seen many times in the Bible, great Sons come from great Fathers. And you are living proof of that fact. The way you have taken up the Mantle of God and added to our father's Legacy is genuinely Glorious. E.L. Gaines' Ministry will continue to save Souls because of your efforts. May God continue to bless you and your wonderful wife, Sheila. Also, I look forward to our future collaboration on your first book.

What can I say about one of the best scholars of the Word of God I have ever met? Elder David Harris has helped me come to a proper understanding of the Bible, absent religion, traditions, and secularism. He has taught me to see beyond the mere Natural and embrace the Spiritual. He has often shared with me what the Body of Christ truly needs in this modern age. He has constantly reminded me of what we, the Church has lost, the true Prophets. Individuals that spoke the truth of God's Word above all else, without fear of consequences. However, Elder Harris may not be entirely right about a fearless Prophet. Let me explain; at certain times while writing this book, I would experience Writer's Block.

Unbeknownst to Elder Harris or me during my Blocks, God would dispatch my dear brother with the words I would need at that time. So, I can say he truly is a Prophet of God without a shadow doubt. May God continue to keep you and your family.

The Bible says God orders the steps of a righteous man. I know this to be true because I crossed paths with this Holy Man of God many years ago in college. Reverend Eric Wells was a young preacher God assigned to our group of boys misbehaving. Eric did his best to keep me and others on the path of righteousness, and as you can see, he succeeded. Later in life, Eric placed his Ministry on hold to assist me with my Church, and I must say what a blessing he has been. Eric was among the most excellent Associate Pastors ever to hold the position. He truly is a laborer for the Lord, and I know he will be rewarded justly one day. God bless you, my friend.

I certainly must acknowledge one of my most supportive family members. Pastor Vera Corley-Sims, what a faithful woman of God. Thank you for all the wisdom, kindness, and love.

You will rarely meet someone in life that is a living example of someone in the Bible. But my uncle Eddie Lee Brown met a Virtuous Woman named Hazel, who has been worth more to him and our family than silver and gold. Many people who have crossed her path will tell you; they were hungry, and she fed them, they were sick, and she comforted them; and they were homeless, and she sheltered them. Here's my testimony about the goodness of this Virtuous Woman. I was out of town when God called my mother Home, my Aunt Hazel was determined not to let my mother depart this life without having a family member by her side. In the middle of the night, she rushed to my mother's bedside and held her hand until she crossed over. Evangelist Hazel Brown, words cannot describe how much you mean to me.

I have been blessed to have met Three Great Educators in my life. Ms. Lucy Tucker, Vice principal Banks, and the Man who placed and kept me on the path, Monroe Ballard. Thank you all.

God sent a very dear person into my life, or, as he would say, a Brother. I must admit, when I first met Russell Waldron, I wasn't behaving very brotherly toward him. But God has a way of placing people in your life that you need. Russell made the writing of this book possible; after all, I am writing it on the MacBook laptop he gave my daughter. Russell and his wife Cindy are so kind and generous, and I know my life would have less joy without them. May God continue to bless and keep you and your loving family, hey Matt.

I have a very dear friend in Phil Mayall; Phil supported my Ministry from the beginning. He is also the photographer who helped with the cover art for this book. You can see his body of work at PhilMFilm.com. Phil and his lovely wife Sharon have been such a blessing to my family. I thank God for the wonderful relationship that has developed between us over the many years.

I don’t have the words to describe what Curtiss Cathey has meant to me. He truly is God-sent; we met many years ago in college. And I have not regretted one day of our journey as we plotted our course to Success. He and his fantastic wife, Renata, have formed an awe-inspiring team. Their marriage is inspirational, and they complement each other. Also, if you can read and understand my book, it is only because Renata is a talented editor. All should remember the name of their company Residential Technology, for it will soon join the ranks of the Fortune 500. I love you guys and look forward to seeing what's next.

I would also like to acknowledge my friend Avery Holt. As I stated throughout the book, I was brought up in the Church, so I view everything through the prism of religion.

I value brother Avery's insight; his views and opinions on life are based on the Human Condition. He stood as an excellent conduit between the secular world and me. Brother Avery, your keen sense of self truly makes you one in a million. Thank you for being you.

Brother Lamont Williams, thank you for all of your help. The advice, support, encouragement, and information were priceless. Also, you can buy his book about building credit on his website. brightlamont.com. May God continue to bless you in all of your endeavors.

All my love to my wonderful sister and brother Mike, Alice, and her husband, Russell. Our father Thomas J. Woods, would have been so proud to see how close we have become. May we continue to spread the kindness and joy he shared with the world.

To everyone else that was such a blessing in my life; Uncle Earl, Aunt Hortense, Aunt Levater, Horace, AWA, Paredes, Adrian, Dinah, Brother, Greg, Tony, Douglas Sligh, Florence, Bruce, Andrew, Ray, Inez family, Chris Mason, Anthony Bell, Larry Curtis, Brodius, Pam, Marcell, Shell, and Simeona Myyone Bleu.

And last but certainly not least. When Adam saw Eve for the first time, he knew there was no other like her in all of Creation. And I share that sentiment; my wife Veda is bone of my bone and flesh of my flesh. I have loved her from the first time I saw her. She has been my First Lady, choir director, soloist, and Church secretary. But more importantly, the mother of my two beloved Angels. Lauren is the eldest and the holder of my Heart. Her birth forever changed my life; she is such a wonderful daughter. She is so curious and intelligent, a chip off the old block. Lauren, I know one day you will make your mark on the world; I love you, my Blessing. Carter is the youngest, and you cannot ask for a better son. He is kind, caring, loving, and so creative.

He has such a great Spirit; to know him is to love him. We actually named him after my wife's family, my grandfather, and a very talented American Poet. And with three names, Carter's personality is still large enough for more. So, I eagerly await to see all the other names that will be bestowed upon him. I love you my Son.

Well everyone, we have come to the end of this particular journey of my life. I have spent the last two years tirelessly studying and researching the Scriptures. I hope you have enjoyed the fruits of my labor. I will end the book like I end my Sermons. If we are a little bit better, the world will be a little bit better. Amen.

REFERENCES

The Holy Bible: King James Version. Thomas Nelson Publisher, Nashville, TN: 1976

The Holy Bible: New International Version. Zondervan Publisher, Grand Rapids, MI: 1984

The Holy Bible and Commentaries. Retrieved from https://www.biblegateway.com

The Holy Bible and Commentaries. Retrieved from https://www.biblehub.org

https://www.biblereason.com

https://www.biblestudytools.com

https://www.cgg.org

https://www.connectusfund.org

https://www.dailyverses.net

https://www.dictionary.cambridge.org

https://www.encyclopedia.britannica.com

https://www.en.m.wikipedia.com

https://www.google.com

https://www.gotquestions.org

https://www.kingjamesbibleonline.org

https://www.knowing-jesus.com

https://www.learn.gcs.edu

https://www.ligonier.org

https://www.merriam-webster.com

https://www.naturallivingfamily.com

https://www.openbible.info

https://outreachjudaism.org

https://www.theconversation.com

https://www.theknot.com

https://www.thesaurus.com

Bible Index

PREFACE

Page ii "I will pour out of my Spirit": Acts 2:17.
Page ii "the whole armour of God": Ephesians 6:11.
Page iii "Here am I; send me": Isaiah 6:8.
Page iii "What doest thou here, Elijah": 1 Kings 19:13.
Page iv "thine heart to understanding": Proverbs 2:2.
Page v "for such a time as this": Esther 4:14.
Page vi "a great multitude": Revelation 7:9.
Page vii "cast thyself down": Matthew 4:6.
Page vii "tempted of Satan": Mark 1:13.
Page vii "all shall be thine": Luke 4:7.
Page viii "But the Comforter": John 14:26.
Page viii "the Holy Ghost": Luke 12:12.
Page ix "forsaking the assembling": Hebrews 10:25.
Page ix "Confess your faults": James 5:16.

INTRODUCTION

Page 01 "Be sober": 1 Peter 5:8.
Page 01 "The thief cometh": John 10:10.
Page 02 "And no marvel": 2 Corinthians 11:14.
Page 03 "there was war in heaven": Revelation 12:7.
Page 03 "I fill heaven and earth": Jeremiah 23:24.
Page 04 "lest thou dash thy foot": Psalms 91:12.
Page 04 "brought down to hell": Isaiah 14:15.
Page 05 "I beheld Satan": Luke 10:18.
Page 05 "hell hath enlarged herself": Isaiah 5:14.
Page 07 "save him from death": Hebrews 5:7.
Page 07 "the Lord of hosts": Zechariah 7:12.

CHAPTER 1

Page 08 “endure sound doctrine”: 2 Timothy 4:3.
Page 09 “a desire to depart”: Philippians 1:22.
Page 10 “a rebellious nation”: Ezekiel 2:3.
Page 10 “a great nation”: Genesis 12:2.
Page 11 “accounted as sheep”: Romans 8:36.
Page 12 “This book of the law”: Joshua 1:7.
Page 13 “the Spirit of truth”: John 14:17.
Page 13 “they deny him”: Titus 1:16.
Page 13 “Let there be light”: Genesis 1:3.
Page 14 “a falling away”: 2 Thessalonians 2:3.
Page 15 “perilous times shall come”: 2 Timothy 3:1.
Page 16 “the engrafted word”: James 1:21.
Page 16 “Cast ye up”: Isaiah 57:14.
Page 16 “Let your light so shine”: Matthew 5:15.
Page 17 “If my people”: 2 Chronicles 7:14.
Page 17 “the Lord filled the house”: 2 Chronicles 7:1.
Page 18 “and without blemish”: Ephesians 5:27.
Page 18 “Moses the servant”: Deuteronomy 34:5
Page 19 “I know thy works”: Revelation 3:1.
Page 19 “for lack of knowledge”: Hosea 4:6.
Page 19 “he is a liar”: 1 John 4:20.
Page 19 “Humble yourself”: James 4:10.
Page 20 “ought always to pray”: Luke 18:11.
Page 20 “ye shall seek me”: Jeremiah 29:13.
Page 20 “whence cometh my help”: Psalm 121:1.
Page 20 “eyes of man”: Proverbs 27:20.
Page 21 “walking on the sea”: Matthew 14:26.
Page 21 “straight before thee”: Proverbs 4:25.
Page 22 “take thine ease”: Luke 12:19.
Page 22 “thou art lukewarm”: Revelations 3:16.
Page 22 “labour is not in vain”: 1 Corinthians 15:58.
Page 22 “to him it is sin”: James 4:17.

Page 22 “return unto me void”: Isaiah 55:11.
Page 23 “Fight the good fight of faith”: 1 Timothy 6:12

CHAPTER 2

Page 24 “the battle is not yours”: 2 Chronicles 20:15.
Page 25 “I was shapen in iniquity”: Psalm 51:5.
Page 25 “all have sinned”: Romans 5:12.
Page 25 “Praise ye the Lord”: Psalm 117:2.
Page 26 “thou shalt not eat”: Genesis 2:17.
Page 26 “that he should lie”: Numbers 23:19.
Page 27 “Let us make man”: Genesis 1:26.
Page 27 “there is none good but one”: Mark 10:18.
Page 27 “it was very good”: Genesis 1:31.
Page 28 “thou art cursed”: Genesis 3:14.
Page 29 “Where art thou”: Genesis 3:8.
Page 29 “A false witness”: Proverbs 6:19.
Page 29 “after mine own heart”: Acts 13:22.
Page 30 “nothing too hard for thee”: Jeremiah 32:17.
Page 30 “thou art mindful of him”: Psalm 8:4.
Page 31 “it repented the Lord”: Genesis 6:6.
Page 31 “Thou art worthy”: Revelation 4:11.
Page 31 “a new heaven”: Revelation 21:1.
Page 32 “Alpha and Omega”: Revelation 21:6.
Page 32 “the tree of life”: Revelation 22:2.
Page 32 “to know good and evil”: Genesis 3:22.
Page 32 “no other gods”: Exodus 20:3.
Page 33 “fainteth not”: Isaiah 40:28.
Page 33 “passed through Macedonia”: Acts 19:21.
Page 33 “be of good cheer”: Acts 27:22.
Page 33 “a viper out of the heat”: Acts 28:3.
Page 33 “the kingdom of God”: Acts 28:31.
Page 34 “Wait on the Lord”: Psalm 27:14.
Page 35 “Spirit of the Lord”: 1 Samuel 16:13.
Page 35 “David was thirty”: 2 Samuel 5:4.

Page 35 “kings of Persia”: Daniel 10:13
Page 36 “after the flesh”: 2 Corinthians 10:3.

CHAPTER 3

Page 37 “iniquity of the fathers”: Numbers 14:18.
Page 39 “to number Israel”: 1 Chronicles 21:1.
Page 41 “risen with Christ”: Colossians 3:1.
Page 41 “so great faith”: Luke 7:9.
Page 42 “Now the serpent”: Genesis 3:1.
Page 42 “knowing good and evil”: Genesis 3:5.
Page 42 “and he died”: Genesis 5:5.
Page 42 “recompense of reward”: Hebrew 2:2.
Page 43 “cursed is the ground”: Genesis 3:17.
Page 43 “thou shalt surely die”: Genesis 2:17.
Page 44 “coats of skins”: Genesis 3:21.
Page 44 “the sin offering”: Leviticus 16:6.
Page 45 “the right hand of God”: Hebrews 10:12.
Page 45 “me and my house”: Joshua 24:15.
Page 45 “and he did eat”: Genesis 3:6.
Page 45 “a tiller of the ground”: Genesis 4:2.
Page 46 “and slew him”: Genesis 4:8.
Page 47 “profit a man”: Mark 8:36.
Page 47 “the wife of Uriah”: 2 Samuel 12:10.
Page 48 “roof of the king’s house”: 2 Samuel 11:2.
Page 48 “Thou shalt not covet”: Exodus 20:17.
Page 48 “Send me Uriah”: 2 Samuel 11:6.
Page 49 “the hand of Uriah”: 2 Samuel 11:14.
Page 49 “dipped the sop”: John 13:26.
Page 50 “will draw all men”: John 12:32.
Page 50 “separate us from the love”: Romans 8:39.
Page 50 “and sin not”: Ephesians 4:26.
Page 50 “Every good gift”: James 1:17.

CHAPTER 4

Page 51 “and defile the man”: Mark 7:23.
Page 52 “shall not inherit”: Galatians 5:21.
Page 52 “But seek ye first”: Matthew 6:33.
Page 52 “O wretched man”: Romans 7:24.
Page 53 “I am the least”: 1 Corinthians 15:9.
Page 53 “be in Christ”: 2 Corinthians 5:17.
Page 53 “this wicked generation”: Matthew 12:45.
Page 54 “I find then a law”: Romans 7:21.
Page 55 “Get thee behind me”: Matthew 16:23.
Page 55 “Woe unto you”: Luke 6:26.
Page 55 “said unto Gideon”: Judges 7:7.
Page 56 “against the prick”: Acts 9:5.
Page 56 “respect of persons”: Romans 2:11.
Page 57 “down to hell”: 2 Peter 2:4.
Page 57 “teach all nations”: Matthew 28:19.
Page 58 “I may win Christ”: Philippians 3:8.
Page 59 “led by the Spirit”: Luke 4:1.
Page 59 “sin unto death”: Romans 6:16.
Page 59 “thirty pieces of silver”: Matthew 27:3.
Page 60 “they took up Jonah”: Jonah 1:15.
Page 60 “after his kind”: Genesis 1:21.
Page 61 “breath of life”: Genesis 2:7.
Page 61 “the devil leaveth him”: Matthew 4:11.
Page 62 “none other name”: Acts 4:12.
Page 62 “thou shalt confess”: Romans 10:9.
Page 62 “strait is the gate”: Matthew 7:14.
Page 63 “Come unto me”: Matthew 11:28.
Page 63 “A sower went out”: Luke 8:5.
Page 64 “murmured against Moses”: Numbers 14:2.
Page 65 “Preach the word”: 2 Timothy 4:2.
Page 65 “house divided”: Matthew 12:25.
Page 65 “of none effect”: Mark 7:13.

Page 66 “Cursed be Canaan”: Genesis 9:25.
Page 66 “Jacob’s well”: John 4:6.
Page 66 “Jew nor Greek”: Galatians 3:28.
Page 67 “I beseech you”: 1 Corinthians 1:10
Page 67 “eaten sour grapes”: Ezekiel 18:2.
Page 68 “hear the word of God”: Luke 8:21.
Page 68 “Casting all your”: 1 Peter 5:7.
Page 68 “greater is he”: 1 John 4:4.
Page 68 “giveth us the victory”: 1 Corinthians 15:57.
Page 69 “Spirit is spirit”: John 3:6.
Page 69 “then an heir”: Galatians 4:7.
Page 69 “a thousand hills”: Psalm 50:10.
Page 69 “the Holy One”: Mark 1:24.
Page 69 “reason together”: Isaiah 1:18.

CHAPTER 5

Page 70 “whom shall we go”: John 6:68.
Page 72 “Peace I leave”: John 14:27.
Page 72 “unequally yoked”: 2 Corinthians 6:14.
Page 73 “peace on earth”: Luke 12:51.
Page 73 “flesh and blood”: Ephesians 6:12.
Page 73 “Son of God”: Mark 15:39.
Page 73 “My sheep hear”: John 10:27.
Page 74 “make us a king”: 1 Samuel 8:5.
Page 74 “good of the land”: Ezra 9:12.
Page 75 “and slew him”: Genesis 4:8.
Page 75 “thy blessing”: Genesis 27:35.
Page 75 “let us sell him”: Genesis 37:27.
Page 75 “And when Delilah”: Judges 16:18.
Page 75 “and kissed him”: Matthew 26:49.
Page 76 “life and peace”: Romans 8:6.
Page 77 “sweet for bitter”: Isaiah 5:20.

Page 77 “armour of God”: Ephesians 6:13.
Page 77 “found with child”: Matthew 1:18.
Page 78 “overcome the world”: John 16:33.
Page 78 “art the Christ”: Matthew 16:16.
Page 78 “author of confusion”: 1 Corinthians 14:33.
Page 78 “from the dead”: Acts 4:10.
Page 79 “ye shall be holy”: Leviticus 20:26.
Page 79 “Study to shew”: 2 Timothy 2:15.
Page 80 “Now faith is”: Hebrews 11:1.
Page 80 “shall it profit”: Mark 8:36.
Page 80 “so loved the world”: John 3:16.
Page 80 “bury my father”: Luke 9:59.
Page 81 “twoedged sword”: Hebrews 4:12.
Page 81 “Pray without ceasing”: 1 Thessalonians 5:17.
Page 82 “not therefore judge”: Romans 14:13.
Page 82 “cast a stone”: John 8:7.

CHAPTER 6

Page 83 “spirit and in truth”: John 4:23.
Page 83 “Let your light”: Matthew 5:16.
Page 84 “holy and profane”: Ezekiel 44:23.
Page 84 “God is a Spirit”: John 4:24.
Page 84 “the Holy Ghost”: Acts 2:38.
Page 84 “flow rivers of living”: John 7:38.
Page 84 “advocate with the”: 1 John 2:1.
Page 84 “every son whom”: Hebrews 12:6.
Page 85 “a wicked man”: Proverbs 6:12.
Page 85 “Judge not”: Matthew 7:1.
Page 86 “with a devil”: Matthew 12:22.
Page 86 “Harden not your”: Hebrews 3:8.
Page 86 “that ask him”: Luke 11:13.
Page 87 “sincere milk of”: 1 Peter 2:2.
Page 87 “fullness of God”: Ephesians 3:19.
Page 87 “works that I do”: John 14:12.

Page 87 “they cannot see” Isaiah 44:18.
Page 88 “the people mourn”: Proverbs 29:2.
Page 88 “believed on Jesus”: John 12:11.
Page 89 “But the Comforter”: John 14:26.
Page 90 “a child is born”: Isaiah 9:6.
Page 90 “son of David”: Matthew 1:1.
Page 90 “repented the Lord”: Genesis 6:6.
Page 90 “But Noah found”: Genesis 6:8.
Page 91 “to all nations”: Romans 16:26.
Page 91 “unto me void”: Isaiah 55:11.
Page 92 “the sons of God”: Job 1:6.
Page 92 “Thy word is true”: Psalm 119:160.
Page 93 “confound their language”: Genesis 11:7.
Page 93 “Daniel answered”: Daniel 5:17.
Page 94 “I am the way”: John 14:6.
Page 94 “mustard seed”: Luke 17:6.
Page 94 “cast into hell”: Luke 12:5.
Page 95 “The Lord is my”: Psalm 23:1
Page 95 “of the beast”: Revelation 13:15.
Page 96 “No weapon”: Isaiah 54:17.
Page 96 “the moneychangers”: Matthew 21:12.
Page 96 “dwell among them”: Exodus 25:8.
Page 97 “prayer and fasting”: Matthew 17:21.
Page 98 “a strong tower”: Proverbs 18:10.
Page 98 “are not carnal”: 2 Corinthians 10:4.
Page 98 “entered Satan into”: Luke 22:3.

CHAPTER 7

Page 99 “power of the tongue”: Proverbs18:21.
Page 99 “strive with man”: Genesis 6:3.
Page 99 “Lazarus is dead”: John 11:14.
Page 99 “the second death”: Revelation 21:8.
Page 100 “in Adam all die”: 1 Corinthians 15:22.
Page 100 “a flaming sword”: Genesis 3:24.

Page 100 “the just shall”: Proverbs 12:13.
Page 100 “by thy words”: Matthew 12:37.
Page 101 “remember me”: Luke 23:42.
Page 101“be made bread”: Luke 4:3.
Page 101 “lose his life”: Matthew 16:25.
Page 101 “Salt is good”: Luke 14:34.
Page 102 “the Son hath life”: 1 John 5:12.
Page 102 “But the tongue”: James 3:8.
Page 102 “be in the faith”: 2 Corinthians 13:5.
Page 103 “made unto salvation”: Romans 10:10.
Page 103 “be born again”: John 3:3.
Page 103 “slow to wrath”: James 1:19.
Page 103 “show us the Father”: John 14:8.
Page 104 “the form of God”: Philippians 2:6.
Page 104 “preaching the gospel”: Matthew 9:35.
Page 104 “and greater works”: John 14:12.
Page 104 “reserved a blessing”: Genesis 27:36.
Page 105 “image of God”: 2 Corinthians 4:4.
Page 105 “the devil said”: Luke 4:3.
Page 105 “Blessed are the”: Matthew 5:9.
Page 105 “children of God”: Galatians 3:26.
Page 105 “heirs of God”: Romans 8:17.
Page 106 “were called Christians”: Acts 11:26.
Page 107 “Jesus I know”: Acts 19:15.
Page 107 “call you blessed”: Malachi 3:12.
Page 108 “not defile himself”: Daniel 1:8.
Page 108 “fiery furnace”: Daniel 3:23.
Page 109 “by their fruits”: Matthew 7:16.

CHAPTER 8

Page 110 “Where art thou”: Genesis 3:9.
Page 110 “call his name Jesus”: Matthew 1:21.
Page 110 “by his grace”: Titus 3:7.
Page 111 “Jesus wept”: John 11:35.

Page 111 “out of sleep”: John 11:11.
Page 112 “so loved the world”: John 3:16.
Page 112 “received him not”: John 1:11.
Page 112 “From that time”: John 6:66.
Page 112 “Martha met him”: John 11:30.
Page 114 “might have light”: John 10:10.
Page 114 “thou art that Christ”: John 6:69.
Page 115 “broad is the way”: Matthew 7:13.
Page 115 “divers temptations”: James 1:2.
Page 115 “love one another”: 1 John 4:7.
Page 116 “bone of my bone”: Genesis 2:23.
Page 116 “at the door”: Revelation 3:20.
Page 116 “love the Lord”: Luke 10:27.
Page 116 “A false balance”: Proverbs 11:1
Page 116 “Train up a child”: Proverbs 22:6.
Page 117 “be in Christ”: 2 Corinthians 5:17.
Page 117 “strait is the gate”: Matthew 7:14.
Page 117 “I am the door”: John 10:9.
Page 117 “eat with publicans”: Mark 2:15.
Page 118 “remember no more”: Hebrews 8:12.
Page 118 “on the heart”: 1 Samuel 16:7.
Page 119 “put my laws”: Hebrews 10:16.
Page 120 “I forgive him”: Matthew 18:21.
Page 120 “shall be given”: Luke 6:38.
Page 121 “death by sin”: Romans 5:12.
Page 121 “adoption of sons”: Galatians 4:5.
Page 122 “house of Israel”: Matthew 15:24.
Page 123 “make you free”: John 8:32.
Page 123 “I am Gabriel”: Luke 1:19.
Page 123 “in the way”: Exodus 23:20.
Page 123 “Praise ye him”: Psalm 148:2.
Page 123 “the Holy One”: Isaiah 40:25.
Page 123 “shalt surely die”: Genesis 2:17.
Page 123 “call upon him”: Psalm 116:2.

CHAPTER 9

Page 124 “is at hand”: Matthew 4:17.
Page 124 “this little child”: Matthew 18:4.
Page 124 “a little child”: Mark 10:15.
Page 124 “a little child”: Luke 18:17.
Page 125 “shall be weeping”: Luke 13:28.
Page 125 “angels of God”: Genesis 28:12.
Page 125 “was the Word”: John 1:1.
Page 126 “he had spoken”: Acts 1:9.
Page 126 “the good wine”: John 2:10.
Page 127 “Our Father”: Luke 11:2.
Page 127 “a chosen generation”: 1 Peter 2:9.
Page 128 “kingdom of God”: 1 Corinthians 4:20.
Page 128 “greater works”: John 14:12.
Page 128 “rather than men”: Acts 5:29.
Page 128 “life is in him”: Acts 20:10.
Page 129 “Now faith”: Hebrews 11:1.
Page 129 “Praying always”: Ephesians 6:18.
Page 130 “foundation of the world”: Ephesian 1:4.
Page 130 “Now Jericho was”: Joshua 6:1.
Page 131 “draw all men”: John 12:32.
Page 131 “day of Pentecost”: Acts 2:1.
Page 131 “my Father”: Matthew 7:21.
Page 131 “like unto a net”: Matthew 13:47.
Page 132 “poor in spirit”: Matthew 5: 3.
Page 132 “keys of the kingdom”: Matthew 16:19.
Page 132 “were added unto”: Acts 2:41.
Page 133 “Good Master”: Matthew 19:16.
Page 134 “of the world”: John 15:19.
Page 135 “in our image”: Genesis 1:26.
Page 135 “their name Adam” Genesis 5:2.
Page 135 “wife’s name Eve” Genesis 3:20.
Page 135 “multiply thy sorrow”: Genesis 3:16.

Page 136 “open the seals”: Revelation 5:9.
Page 137 “put on Christ”: Galatians 3:27.
Page 137 “present you holy”: Colossians 1:22.
Page 137 “we shall reign”: Revelations 5:10.
Page 137 “Touch me not”: John 20:17.
Page 137 “a true saying”: 1 Timothy 3:1.
Page 138 “shall be saved”: Romans 10:13.
Page 138 “to the plough”: Luke 9:62.
Page 139 “free from sin”: Romans 6:7.
Page 139 “Go ye therefore”: Matthew 28:19.
Page 139 “not the world”: 1 John 2:15.
Page 141 “all gone aside”: Psalm 14:3.
Page 141 “out of course”: Psalm 82:5.
Page 142 “the solid rock”: 1 Corinthians 3:10.
Page 142 “suffering the vengeance”: Jude 1:7.
Page 143 “let them marry”: 1Corinthians 7:9.
Page 143 “cannot please God”: Romans 8:8.
Page 144 “sound doctrine”: Titus 2:1.
Page 144 “way of wisdom”: Proverbs 4:11.
Page 144 “the righteous forsaken”: Psalm 37:25.
Page 145 “from the cross”: Matthew 27:42.
Page 145 “signs and wonders”: John 4:48.
Page 145 “Rest in the Lord”: Psalm 37:7.
Page 145 “make one wise”: Genesis 3:6.
Page 145 “walk by faith”: 2 Corinthians 5:7.
Page 145 “But without faith”: Hebrews 11:6.
Page 145 “Joshua blessed him”: Joshua 14:13.
Page 146 “dwelt therein”: Joshua 19:50.
Page 146 “only begotten Son”: 1 John 4:9.
Page 146 “A new commandment”: John 13:34.
Page 146 “in uncertain riches”: 1 Timothy 6:17.
Page 147 “call upon God”: Psalm 55:16.
Page 147 “right unto a man”: Proverbs 16:25.
Page 147 “the potter’s Jeremiah 18:6.

Page 147 “the whole lump”: Galatians 5:9.
Page 148 “Ye cannot drink”: 1 Corinthians 10:21.
Page 148 “it is written”: Romans 14:11.
Page 149 “Every wise woman”: Proverbs 14:1.
Page 149 “issues of life”: Proverbs 4:23.

CHAPTER 10

Page 150 “grinding at the mill”: Matthew 24:41.
Page 151 “sign of thy coming”: Matthew 24:3.
Page 155 “a falling away”: 2 Thessalonians 2:3.
Page 156 “Hell from beneath”: Isaiah 14:9.
Page 157 “shew thyself approved”: 2 Timothy 2:15.
Page 157 “cast out devils”: Matthew 7:22.
Page 157 “bought with a price”: 1 Corinthians 6:20.
Page 158 “eat the flesh”: John 6:53.
Page 158 “the Lord answered Job”: Job 38:1.
Page 159 “is born this day”: Luke 2:11.
Page 159 “of the forest”: Jeremiah 10:3.
Page 160 “thine own eye”: Luke 6:41.
Page 160 “is for us”: Luke 9:50.
Page 161 “corner stone”: Isaiah 28:16.
Page 161 “upon this rock”: Matthew 16:18.
Page 161 “for ye know not”: Mark 13:33.
Page 161 “the Holy One”: Mark 1:24.
Page 162 “when Jesus was born”: Matthew 2:1.
Page 163 “false prophets”: Mark 13:22.
Page 163 “rest with us”: 2 Thessalonians 1:7.
Page 164 “appeared to all men” Titus 2:11.
Page 164 “the days of methuselah”: Genesis 5:27.
Page 164 “and great commandment”: Matthew 22:38.
Page 165 “dust of the ground”: Genesis 2:7.
Page 165 “And the rib”: Genesis 2:22.
Page 165 “took of the fruit”: Genesis 3:6.
Page 165 “Noah found grace”: Genesis 6:8.

Page 166 “book of the law”: Joshua 1:8.
Page 166 “only begotten Son”: John 3:16.
Page 166 “he is risen”: Mark 16:6.
Page 166 “and prepare a place”: John 14:3.
Page 166 “with other tongues”: Acts 2:4.
Page 167 “And this gospel”: Matthew 24:14.
Page 167 “Ye are the salt”: Matthew 5:13.
Page 167 “Watch ye therefore”: Luke 21:36.

ABOUT THE AUTHOR

Pastor Vincent Woods grew up in the Church. As a young man, he served in many different departments at his home Church, New Macedonia Missionary Baptist. He sang in the youth choir. Eventually, he was ordained as a Deacon and later Chairman of the Deacon Board. He also taught Sunday School and Bible Study Classes. God later moved Vincent into Ministry, serving as Assistant Pastor to the late M.J. Johnson. From there, he founded and served as Pastor of Victory Baptist Church until he was called to Pastor Inez Baptist Church. Pastor Woods loves to study and it shows. His educational background is extensive; he has majored in History, Business Administration, and Biology. He also has Minors in Psychology and Sociology. Reverend Woods is currently pursuing a Degree in Religious Studies. Vincent has worked for several Fortune 500 Companies in the private sector, mainly in transportation. Vincent has owned many Businesses, including a Subway Sandwich Shop franchise. Pastor Woods has been married for nineteen years to his lovely wife, Veda. They have two wonderful children, Lauren and Carter. One of Pastor Woods lifelong dreams was to become an Author, and now God has brought that dream to reality. What a joyous blessing.

Made in the USA
Columbia, SC
27 July 2024